Q is for Quark

A Science Alphabet Book

Written by David M. Schwartz
Illustrated by Kim Doner

–Do YOU know what a quark is?

–Does it matter?

–Hey– it IS <u>matter</u>!

Quark! Quark! QUARK! Hey, I like the sound of THAT!

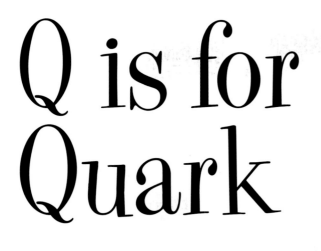

Tricycle Press
Berkeley | Toronto

To the fabulous folks at Tricycle Press, and especially to
Nicole Geiger and Christine Longmuir who are everything
an author could hope for, and more. Thank you from
the bottom of my quarks. —D.S.

This book is for my favorite
Number One Quarkster, David Schwartz.
F is for Friendship! —K.D.

Text copyright © 2001 by David Schwartz
Illustrations © 2001 by Kim Doner

TRICYCLE PRESS
P.O. Box 7123
Berkeley, California 94707
www.tenspeed.com

Text design by Tasha Hall
Cover design by Jean Sanchirico

This book was set in Bodoni Book, Pike, and MetaPlus.

Library of Congress Cataloging-in-Publication Data

Schwartz, David M.
   Q is for quark : a science alphabet book / written by David M. Schwartz ; illustrated
by Kim Doner.
      p. cm.
   ISBN 1-58246-021-3
   1. Science—Miscellanea—Juvenile literature. 2. Alphabet—Juvenile literature.
[1. Science—Miscellanea. 2. Alphabet.] I. Doner, Kim, 1955– ill. II. Title.
Q173 .S393 2001
500—dc21   00-010659

First printing, 2001
Printed in Hong Kong
1 2 3 4 5 6 7 — 06 05 04 03 02 01

Content**S**

Acknowledgments

David Schwartz and Tricycle Press would like to thank the following people for their invaluable participation in the production of this book:

Glenn Cantor, D.V.M., Ph.D., and Inge Eriks, D.V.M., Ph.D., College of Veterinary Medicine, Washington State University, Pullman, WA; Emma Cantor, budding scientist, 5th grader; Alida Cantor, 9th grader

Barbara Ehrlich, Ph.D., professor of Pharmacology, Yale University School of Medicine, New Haven, CT

James Griesemer, Ph.D., professor of Philosophy, University of California, Davis, CA

John Hayes, Ph.D., professor of Biochemistry, Marlboro College, Marlboro, VT

Melinda Holtzman, instructor in Electrical Engineering, University of Nevada, Reno, NV; intructor in Physics, Truckee Meadows Community College, Reno, NV

Brigid Kane, freelance science writer and editor, Gloversville, NY

Leo Kretzner, Ph.D., research scientist, The City of Hope National Medical Center, Duarte, CA

Christine Laddish, science teacher, Head-Royce School, Oakland, CA

Ann E. Mallard, instructor in Biology, City College of San Francisco, San Francisco, CA

Barbara Marinak, reading/federal programs coordinator, Central Dauphin School District, Harrisburg, PA

Sarah Martin, kids' science editor, Sebastopol, CA

Lynn Redpath, 6th grade teacher, and Tyler Wolf, 7th grade student, Paris Gibson Middle School, Great Falls, MT

Susan L. Scott, library/media specialist, Rio Linda Union School District, Sacramento, CA

Paul Vetter, Ph.D., staff scientist, E.O. Lawrence Berkeley National Laboratory, Berkeley, CA

Denise White, 6th grade teacher, Language Arts, DuPont Middle School, Belle, WV

John Zawadzki, Ph.D., president, BioMed Communications and consultant to the pharmaceutical industry, New York, NY

A is for Atom

Suppose you took a cookie and cut it into little pieces, and then you cut those pieces into crumbs and those crumbs into littler and littler crumbs, and so on. Would you ever get to a point where it became impossible—no matter how good your knife, your hand, or your eyes—to cut any further? Would you ever reach the smallest possible piece of cookie? Or could you keep dividing it into smaller and smaller cookie bits…forever?

The ancient Greek philosophers wondered about things like this. One fellow, Democritus, said that all matter (that's what scientists call the "stuff" of the world) was made of tiny bits. He called these bits *atoms*, from the Greek word for "not cuttable." He believed the bits were put together in different ways to make different kinds of matter. Another philosopher, Aristotle, didn't think matter came in bits. He thought it all flowed together, like water running through your fingers.

Well, it turns out that Democritus was right. But it took many more centuries for scientists to prove the existence of atoms. They have since identified about 90 different kinds of atoms that occur naturally. Atoms are the building blocks of all matter. Matter can be made up of just one kind of atom, or different kinds of atoms joined together.

Atoms are tiny. A million atoms stacked on top of one another wouldn't be quite as thick as a hair on your head. About 100 billion of them would cover the period at the end of this sentence. An atom is so small that a single drop of water contains more than a million million billion atoms. That's 1,000,000,000,000,000,000,000! Of course their exact size depends on the atom. Some are smaller, some bigger. The smallest kind of atom is hydrogen, which also happens to be the most abundant atom in the universe. Uranium is the largest kind of atom, except for a few really big ones that scientists have made in laboratories.

Most of the time, atoms really are "not cuttable," as Democritus said. But scientists have special ways of breaking them apart in order to study them. (Please don't try this at home.) They have found that atoms themselves are made up of smaller parts.

Most of the space in an atom is a "cloud" of incredibly tiny *electrons*. Electrons whiz around at millions of miles per hour (and yet never get stopped for speeding). Because the electrons are going so fast, they're practically everywhere at once, and so scientists think of them as a cloud.

THE GREAT DEBATE!
(IT WAS ALL GREEK TO THEM)

—The tiniest "bit" is an atom. For instance, URANIUM is **not** cuttable!

—My WHAT?

—Uranium. It's not cuttable.

—Well, I would hope NOT!

Hey, check this out! 100,000,000,000 atoms, right here on this period. And that one! And over there!

How can you write a ticket for something that's everywhere at once?

5

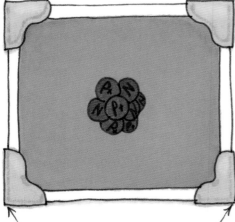

The Atomic Nucleus
(enlarged)

The darker areas are where an electron is most likely to be found.

Clouds of Probability
Electrons are so small and fast, scientists can only figure where they PROBABLY are around an atomic nucleus.

Somewhere deep inside the electron cloud is a *nucleus*. If the electron cloud were the size of a baseball stadium, the nucleus—floating somewhere in the middle of the stadium—would be smaller than the baseball. The nucleus of an atom is made from two types of particles—*protons* and *neutrons*. They give the atom almost all of its *mass* (that's a measure of how much matter is in something—see **G is for Gravity**).

Aside from mass, there's another big difference between an atom's electron cloud and its nucleus. The electrons have a negative electric charge, and the nucleus has a positive charge. Actually, it's the protons in the nucleus that are positively charged. As their name suggests, the neutrons are neutral (they have no charge). These positive and negative charges hold the atom together. This is because things with unlike charges are attracted to each other, while things with the same charge repel each other. (If you've ever played with magnets, you know that the negative and positive poles of two magnets are eager to know each other and you can tell because they stick together when they get close, but you can't force the two negative poles or the two positive poles to get personal.) An atom has an equal number of positive and negative charges, so it must have the same number of protons in its nucleus as electrons outside the nucleus.

The number of protons in the nucleus of an atom is called the *atomic number*, and since we know an atom is neutral, the atomic number also tells us the number of electrons outside its nucleus. A hydrogen atom has one proton and one electron, so its atomic number is 1. An oxygen atom has eight protons and eight electrons, for an atomic number of 8. With 47 protons and 47 electrons, silver has an atomic number of…you figure it out! Scientists organize atoms according to their atomic number (see **E is for Element**). Depending on how many protons and electrons they have, atoms behave in different ways, just like people—except atoms are easier to predict than people!

Though it appears that the electrons of an atom form a cloud around the nucleus, it turns out that there are actually "mini-clouds" within the big cloud. The mini-clouds are called *shells*. Each shell holds a different number of electrons. The first shell (which is closest to the nucleus) can hold 2, the second can hold 8, the third can

Vat? Tryink to sneak op in ze line again? Beck in place, Mr. Oxygen!

Rats! I thought farther up in line meant less WAIT, not less weight!

You're wrong twice- atomic number is NOT atomic weight!

That Oxygen! What an airhead.

Tch-tch! Hardly model behavior.

Yes- such a BOHR!

HEY! That's MY place!

H¹ He² Li³ Be⁴ B⁵ C⁶ N⁷ O⁸ F⁹ Ne⁸

hold 18, and the fourth can hold 32. These numbers turn out to be really important because atoms "want" to have their outer shells completely full or completely empty, and they are always trying to fill or empty them. (Of course electrons aren't human and they don't have feelings or desires, but they are definitely strong-willed when it comes to filling or emptying their shells.)

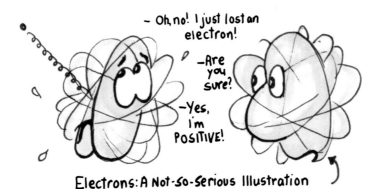

- Oh, no! I just lost an electron!

- Are you sure?

- Yes, I'm POSITIVE!

Electrons: A Not-So-Serious Illustration

Atoms fill or empty their shells by finding other atoms to give electrons to, or accept electrons from, or share electrons with. When two or more atoms get together to share electrons, the result is a molecule and the process is called a chemical reaction. An entire branch of science, chemistry, is devoted to studying what happens when atoms get to know each other.

Since the nucleus of an atom is like a ball inside a stadium, and since practically all the matter of an atom is in its nucleus, an atom is mostly empty space. And since you're made of atoms and the chair you're sitting on is made of atoms and the floor the chair is resting on is made of atoms and the earth supporting the floor is made of atoms and so forth…you might be wondering this: Why don't you (mostly empty space) just fall right through the chair (mostly empty space) and continue falling through the floor (mostly empty space) and the earth (mostly empty space)? If you weren't wondering, please start wondering now!

The answer is electrons. Though an atom is mostly empty space, that space has negatively charged electrons whizzing through it all the time. The electrons of the chair are negatively charged and the electrons of your bottom are also negatively charged. Remember what we said about opposite charges attracting and like charges repelling? Because the negative charges of your bottom are in contact with the negative charges of the chair, they push against each other. So, you stay on the chair. It's a good thing, too, because it would be hard to read this book while plunging toward the center of the earth.

Electrons: A Serious Illustration

2 8 18 32

If I could get all of the electrons out of this broccoli, would it fall to the center of the earth BEFORE dinner?

…and A is also for

absolute zero

air pressure (also
    called atmospheric
    pressure)

amoeba

atmosphere

atomic weight

axon

WHO just called me a "BALL of HOT GAS"?

B is for Black Hole

Stars are born every day. Like people, these balls of hot gas grow up, get older, and eventually die. Unlike people, stars are big when they are young, and get smaller as they age. Inside a young star, hydrogen atoms crash into each other to form helium. The process is called *nuclear fusion*, and it releases huge amounts of *energy*. We see some of that energy as light. If we're close enough to the star, as we are with our Sun, we can also feel the energy as heat.

For its entire life, a star is a battle zone. Its own huge *gravitational force* not only attracts anything nearby, but also pulls the star itself inward, trying to crush it into a super-dense, super-small mass. (See **G is for Gravity**.) At the same time, the star's nuclear engine gives off a huge amount of energy that pushes outward, counteracting the inward force of the star's own gravity. As a result, the star neither explodes nor collapses.

That's all well and good while the star is bright and shining. But what happens when it starts to run out of hydrogen? Now there's a lot less energy being given off to counteract the gravitational force pulling inward. Eventually, the star collapses. How much does it collapse? That depends on how much mass it has. What happens is the opposite of what you might expect: Because the largest living stars have the greatest gravitational pull, they collapse to become the smallest when they die.

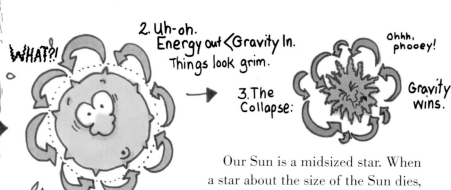

Ah! Life is good!

WHAT?!

2. Uh-oh. Energy out < Gravity In. Things look grim.

3. The Collapse:

Ohhh, phooey!

Gravity wins.

1. Bright and Shining: Energy Out ≈ Gravity In.

Our Sun is a midsized star. When a star about the size of the Sun dies, its gravitational force turns it into a heap of ash about the size of the Earth. Considering how large it was to begin with (you could fit a million Earths into the Sun), that makes for a pretty dense mass of stuff. A golfball-sized hunk of the ash would weigh more than a million elephants. (Golf caddies had better start working out!) But that's nothing compared to what happens when a truly massive star

And now, the sequel:

The Death of A Star (An Inside Story)

1. Fresh out of gas: Gravity rules.

Electrons are pushed into atomic nuclei.

Hey! Quit shoving!

Bully!

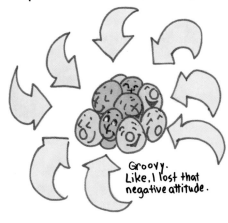

2. The force is with them: They react with protons to become neutrons.

Groovy. Like, I lost that negative attitude.

collapses, the pressures are so enormous that the star's electrons get shoved into the nuclei of its atoms ("nuclei" is the plural of "nucleus"), where they react with the protons to form neutrons. The star, now made mostly of jammed-together neutrons, is called a *neutron star*. A neutron star is squeezed together so tightly that a golfball-sized piece of it would weigh about as much as a billion elephants! (Golf caddies had better find another line of work!)

When the most massive stars of all collapse, their gravitational pull becomes so tremendous that nothing can escape them, not even light. (See **L is for Light.**) Thus they are invisible, and are called *black holes*. Anything and everything that comes near a black hole—gas, dust, light, astronauts—gets sucked in, never to be seen again. A black hole is not a good vacation destination.

If you're wondering how light can be "sucked in" by gravity, think of it this way: On Earth, it's possible to escape the pull of gravity if you can travel fast enough—about 11 kilometers (7 miles) per second. This speed, called Earth's *escape velocity*, is how fast a spaceship must go in order to be launched. A black hole has such tremendous gravitational pull that its escape velocity is more than the speed of light, which is 300,000 kilometers (186,000 miles) per second. Nothing can go faster than light—not even light (of course!). That's why a black hole is black. So how do we know it's there?

In 1970, the satellite Uhuru encountered a star called Cygnus 1 that behaved as though it were being dragged around by something that couldn't be seen. The invisible something seemed to have the gravitational pull of 10 Suns and it appeared to be tearing gas away from the star. Yet, despite gobbling up all that glowing gas, the invisible something did not glow.

That "something" was the first good evidence of a black hole. Since then, the Hubble Space Telescope has provided even more convincing evidence for black holes. Some astronomers believe there are supermassive black holes made from millions of collapsed stars lurking at the center of every galaxy. There may also be mini black holes the size of pencil points or peas! And some think that black holes are "doorways" to other universes. We'll walk through that door, but only with a *round-trip* ticket, please!

The packed protons and neutrons become a neutron star. It sucks up everything, including:

HOMEWORK!

...and B is also for

bacterium

barometer

biome

boil

bond

I'm woolly, woolly famous!
I'm woolly, woolly famous!
People flock to see me!
People flock to see me!

A simple case of déjà ewe?

...and C is also for

cell

chemical bond

chemical reaction

cold-blooded

compound

condense

covalent bond

C is for Clone

Warning: Do not read this…yet! Read **D is for DNA** first. Yes, we know that C comes before D, but you have to understand DNA before you can understand what a clone is. Hey, we didn't invent the alphabet.

Have you heard of Dolly? We don't mean Dolly Madison or Dolly Parton. We're talking about Dolly the sheep. She is the most famous sheep in the world, and all she did to become so famous was to be born. Dolly's birth was international news, because Dolly is a *clone*.

A clone is a living thing that has exactly the same *genes* as its parent. Genetically speaking, Dolly is an identical copy of her mother. That's not true for you. Like everyone else in the world, you get half your genes from your mother and half from your father. Unless you have an identical twin, there is no one with your same exact set of genes. The same applied to sheep—until Dolly.

Scientists in Scotland cloned Dolly by taking the nucleus out of a *cell* from one female sheep, and using it to replace the nucleus of a fertilized egg removed from a second sheep. This egg was then put into the uterus of a third sheep, where it developed into a normal, healthy newborn lamb. The sheep that gave birth to Dolly was not her mother. Dolly's mom was the first sheep, the one who "donated" a cell nucleus (not that she offered to make a donation).

Dolly wasn't the first clone. Strawberries and many other plants produce "runners" that are actually clones, and grow into new plants. One-celled amoebas divide in half to make two genetically identical animals, clones of each other. Identical copies of humanmade things can be called clones—you might not have to look far to find some.

But Dolly was the first mammal to be cloned, and no sooner had Dolly uttered her first "baaaah" than some people responded with "Baaaah Humbug!" A worldwide debate continues to rage over whether or not cloning is a good thing. Lots of people worry that cloning humans is next, which they view as morally wrong. Who would get to decide which people could be cloned? What would stop a very rich person from making many clones of himself or herself?

On the other side of the debate, some people think cloning humans would be great. Through cloning, you could achieve a sort of "immortality" as a young "you" started all over! And even if we didn't clone whole people, we could clone organs and tissues from the same people who need them for transplants. This way there would be no problem with organ rejection. (See **I is for Immune System.**)

Both sides have good points. What do you think?

I'm woolly, woolly famous!
I'm woolly, woolly famous!
People flock to see me!
People flock to see me!

WARNING:
DOLLY
REPEATS
HERSELF

A simple case of déjà ewe?

...and C is also for

cell

chemical bond

chemical reaction

cold-blooded

compound

condense

covalent bond

C is for Clone

Warning: Do not read this…yet! Read **D is for DNA** first. Yes, we know that C comes before D, but you have to understand DNA before you can understand what a clone is. Hey, we didn't invent the alphabet.

Have you heard of Dolly? We don't mean Dolly Madison or Dolly Parton. We're talking about Dolly the sheep. She is the most famous sheep in the world, and all she did to become so famous was to be born. Dolly's birth was international news, because Dolly is a *clone*.

A clone is a living thing that has exactly the same *genes* as its parent. Genetically speaking, Dolly is an identical copy of her mother. That's not true for you. Like everyone else in the world, you get half your genes from your mother and half from your father. Unless you have an identical twin, there is no one with your same exact set of genes. The same applied to sheep—until Dolly.

Scientists in Scotland cloned Dolly by taking the nucleus out of a *cell* from one female sheep, and using it to replace the nucleus of a fertilized egg removed from a second sheep. This egg was then put into the uterus of a third sheep, where it developed into a normal, healthy newborn lamb. The sheep that gave birth to Dolly was not her mother. Dolly's mom was the first sheep, the one who "donated" a cell nucleus (not that she offered to make a donation).

Dolly wasn't the first clone. Strawberries and many other plants produce "runners" that are actually clones, and grow into new plants. One-celled amoebas divide in half to make two genetically identical animals, clones of each other. Identical copies of humanmade things can be called clones—you might not have to look far to find some.

But Dolly was the first mammal to be cloned, and no sooner had Dolly uttered her first "baaaah" than some people responded with "Baaaah Humbug!" A worldwide debate continues to rage over whether or not cloning is a good thing. Lots of people worry that cloning humans is next, which they view as morally wrong. Who would get to decide which people could be cloned? What would stop a very rich person from making many clones of himself or herself?

On the other side of the debate, some people think cloning humans would be great. Through cloning, you could achieve a sort of "immortality" as a young "you" started all over! And even if we didn't clone whole people, we could clone organs and tissues from the same people who need them for transplants. This way there would be no problem with organ rejection. (See **I is for Immune System**.)

Both sides have good points. What do you think?

- I'm so sorry. It appears that your son...is a pine tree.
- Oh, Doctor! How could you tell?
- I could see it in his genes.

I've got FIR to go...

A Single Cell

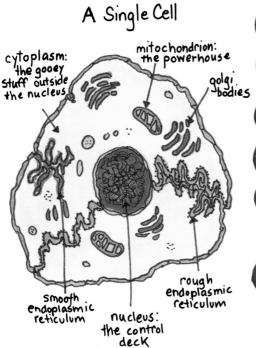

cytoplasm: the gooey stuff outside the nucleus

mitochondrion: the powerhouse

golgi bodies

smooth endoplasmic reticulum

nucleus: the control deck

rough endoplasmic reticulum

D is for DNA

Here's a secret code for you:

CTGAATTCAGAAAGCTTGACAGTCTTGACG

Can you crack the code? This impossible-sounding string of C's, T's, G's and A's may look like total gibberish, but these letters are part of the secret code that made YOU! Well, the whole code is a lot longer (about 3 billion letters long), so this is just a tiny piece of it. And we don't know exactly what your particular code is, but we do know that part of it is very similar to what's written above. And so is the code that made your best friend. And your worst enemy. And your cat. And the mouse your cat just ate. And the bush where the mouse was hiding just before the cat came along. And the mold on the leaves of the bush. And just about every other living thing that ever lived. This code is called *DNA*.

DNA stands for *deoxyribonucleic acid*. It's the secret of life. It determines whether you are a human or a pine tree, and it determines a great deal about just what kind of human (or pine tree) you are.

All living things are made of cells. Some organisms (that's what biologists call living things) consist of just one cell. They can do everything they need to do with just one cell, but it is absolutely impossible for them to read a book or juggle rubber balls or bake cookies. Other organisms, like you, have trillions of cells.

Cells are filled with jelly-like stuff called *cytoplasm*, and through-out the cytoplasm are tiny structures called *organelles*. In the center of every cell is a large nucleus (not to be confused with an atomic nucleus). Think of a cell as a living factory, and the nucleus as the cell's "command center." Inside the nucleus are threadlike things made of DNA molecules called *chromosomes*. Chromosomes come in pairs. In every human cell (except sperm and egg cells) there are 23 pairs of chromosomes—46 chromosomes in all.

The DNA molecules in chromosomes are very long and very thin, but they are tightly wound around themselves many times. If you could unwind the strands of DNA and bunch them like a cable, five million of them could fit through the eye of a needle. Stretched out in a line, the DNA from one cell would be taller than most adults (but not quite as tall as a pro basketball player).

While you've got your DNA unwound, you might as well take a look at it. Magnify it 50 million times. Now you can see that it looks a lot like a spiral ladder that scientists call a *double helix*. It has side pieces, or strands, and rungs connecting the strands. The important thing about this spiral ladder is the rungs. They are made of groups of atoms called *DNA bases*. There are four kinds of bases: adenine, thymine, guanine, and cytosine. Just call them A, T, G, and C. Each rung is made up of two bases attached to each other. Now here's the important part: DNA bases are very fussy about who they attach to. C attaches only to G (and G only to C). Neither C nor G would ever dream of attaching to A or T. But A and T are just as fussy. They attach only to each other.

It's amazing what all this fussiness means. Take a look at the "secret code" on the previous page. Because you now know how the DNA bases bond with each other, you can figure out what bases would be on the opposing strand. Remember that A and T go together, and C and G go together. So the base pairs in this part of the double helix would look like this:

CTGAATTCAGAAAGCTTGACAGTCTTGACG
GACTTAAGTCTTTCGAACTGTCAGAACTGC

Of course it doesn't end there. We are showing you just a small segment of a DNA molecule that might exist.

When a cell divides to create two cells, the DNA molecules "unzip." Here's what you get:

CTGAATTCAGAAAGCTTGACAGTCTTGACG

GACTTAAGTCTTTCGAACTGTCAGAACTGC

All of this takes place in the cell's nucleus where lots of lonely single bases are floating around, looking for others to attach to. When the DNA molecule unzips, it exposes bases that the lonely ones can attach to. They're not lonely for long! Here's what they look like after they've found mates.

CTGAATTCAGAAAGCTTGACAGTCTTGACG
GACTTAAGTCTTTCGAACTGTCAGAACTGC

CTGAATTCAGAAAGCTTGACAGTCTTGACG
GACTTAAGTCTTTCGAACTGTCAGAACTGC

So now you've got two identical copies of the same sequence of base pairs. The cell has duplicated its DNA. (Cells knew how to do this long before photocopy machines were invented.) This way, when the cell divides into two daughter cells (we don't know why they're never called "son" cells), each daughter receives an identical copy of DNA.

The traits that you inherited from your parents are coded in the groups of base pairs, called genes, that make up your parents' DNA. Those A's, T's, G's and C's determine whether you'll be short or tall, have blue eyes or brown eyes, blonde hair or black hair, long legs or

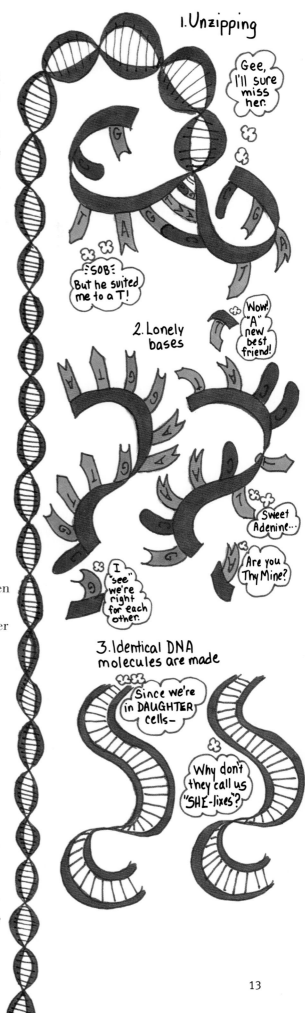

Groups of DNA base pairs make up genes. Tens of thousands of genes make up each human chromosome.

Wow! Eggzactly what I wanted!

Egg and sperm cells have 23 chromosomes apiece...

and when the cells join...

those chromosomes meet...

and replicate over and over in cells that divide...

and grow into YOU!

Moi?

...and D is also for

decibel

density

diffraction

short legs, and thousands of other things. They also determine whether you will be susceptible to certain diseases that can be inherited. (Some people believe your intelligence and many aspects of your personality are also inherited though your parents' DNA. Others think those things depend more on what happens to you after you're born—your experiences and how you were raised. Still others think it's both!)

When sperm cells were made inside your father's body and egg cells were made inside your mother's body, each one got 23 chromosomes, or half of each parent's DNA. When your father's sperm fertilized your mother's egg, the cell formed by the two of them now had 46 chromosomes—the full amount of DNA needed to make you. As that cell divided and divided until you were born, the DNA kept on duplicating, so that every single one of the billions of cells in your body has the same exact DNA—half from your mother and half from your father.

Your DNA continues to work for you every second of every day. Each of the trillions of tiny cells in your body is a little factory, and the DNA in each of those cells is the blueprint that runs the factory. Whatever the cell, whatever the species, DNA is the master plan of life. If you could rearrange all those A's, T's, G's and C's that make up your DNA, you could be Einstein. Or a slime mold.

E is for Element

Exploro, an alien from the planet Scientifica, has arrived on Earth to explore a small portion of our planet to determine what sorts of things are found here. Exploro's study site: your bedroom.

Here is a list of everything our friendly but curious alien collects from your room and brings back to Scientifica. Exploro believes these objects are the building blocks of everything else on Earth.

Empty Soda Can	Stickers
Pennies	Paper Clips
Gummy Bears	Shoelaces
Popcorn	Plastic Bag
Sunflower Seeds	Paper
Candle Wax	Fiberfill
Diamond Earring	Dust Balls
Buttons	Pizza
T-Shirt	Deodorant

In a laboratory back in Scientifica, Exploro closely examines the items in your room and realizes that some of them, like paper clips and pennies and your diamond, seem to be made of only one substance while others, like pizza and sunflower seeds, and dust balls, seem to be made of more substances. Shoelaces, for instance, have both fabric and plastic. Popcorn is made of butter and salt and corn. Stickers are made of paper and glue and ink. Pizza is made of…well, you get the idea. And with further analysis he sees that many of these substances are made of even more basic ingredients. Butter is made of water and fat with some milk solids thrown in. After heating, cooling, burning, mixing, squeezing, dissolving, spinning, and other procedures, Exploro finds that everything he collected is made from about 30 very basic substances. Among them are hydrogen, oxygen, nitrogen, silicon, carbon, iron, sodium, calcium, and silver. These, Exploro believes, are the true *elements* of Earth.

Exploro didn't find all of Earth's elements in your room, but aside from that, he is right. An element is something that cannot be broken down into simpler substances. It is made of only one kind of atom. (See **A is for Atom.**) The ancient Greeks thought that everything was made of water, air, earth, or fire. Boy, were they off! We now know that none of those is actually an element, but there are about 90 true elements that occur naturally on Earth. No two elements can be combined to form another element.

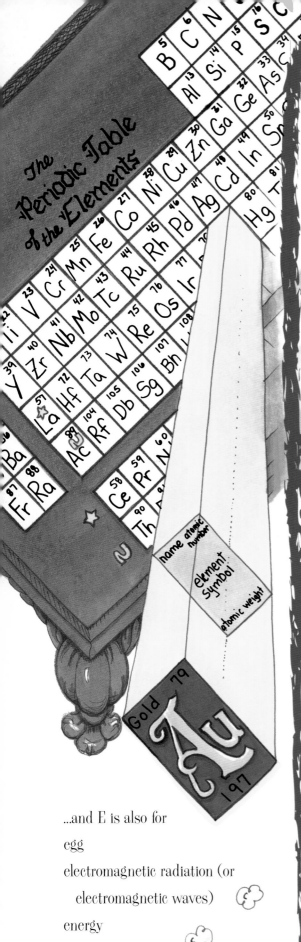

The Periodic Table of the Elements

name   atomic number

element symbol

atomic weight

Gold 79

Au

197

Even though elements cannot be combined to form other elements, two or more elements can combine to make something else, called a *compound*. The smallest bit of a compound you could possibly have is a *molecule*. For example, two atoms of the element hydrogen (H) and one atom of the element oxygen (O) make one molecule of water, H_2O. Some gigantic molecules, like DNA, contain thousands of atoms.

In the 18th century, chemists began to think about ways to organize the growing list of elements they had discovered. They looked at the atomic number (the number of protons of one atom) of each element and realized that if they put them in order, starting with hydrogen (atomic number 1), then helium (atomic number 2), then lithium (atomic number 3), and so forth, something interesting happened: As you went through the elements one by one, their chemical properties changed gradually, but then the pattern repeated. It's sort of like a song where the words change with each verse, but the tune repeats.

Modern chemists have organized all the elements into a chart that makes them a lot easier to understand. The chart is called the *Periodic Table of the Elements*. It shows the abbreviation for each element and a lot of information, but the real beauty of it is that it shows a pattern and lets us predict chemical reactions. For instance, lithium, in the far left column, reacts violently with water. You don't want to be near the chemist who lets his lithium get wet. Sodium and potassium are also found in the far left row, and they also react explosively with water. Over in the next-to-last column of the table, you'll find oxygen. As you know (or if you don't, see **H is for H_2O**), single atoms of oxygen like to combine with two atoms of hydrogen to create H_2O, or water. Sulfur, found below oxygen, also combines with two atoms of hydrogen to form hydrogen sulfide, H_2S, the smelly stuff that gives rotten eggs (and mineral waters) their odor. All the elements in the far right row are known as inert, or noble, gases. *Inert* means "doesn't do anything." (Maybe they're also called "noble" because an 18th century chemist didn't think the "noble" aristocrats did much either!)

Exploro is pleased with the Earth elements he found on his first trip. But he'd like to find more, so he's coming back. This time he's going to explore your sister's room.

...and E is also for

egg

electromagnetic radiation (or electromagnetic waves)

energy

enzyme

I wonder if deodorant tastes as good as pizza?

F is for Fault

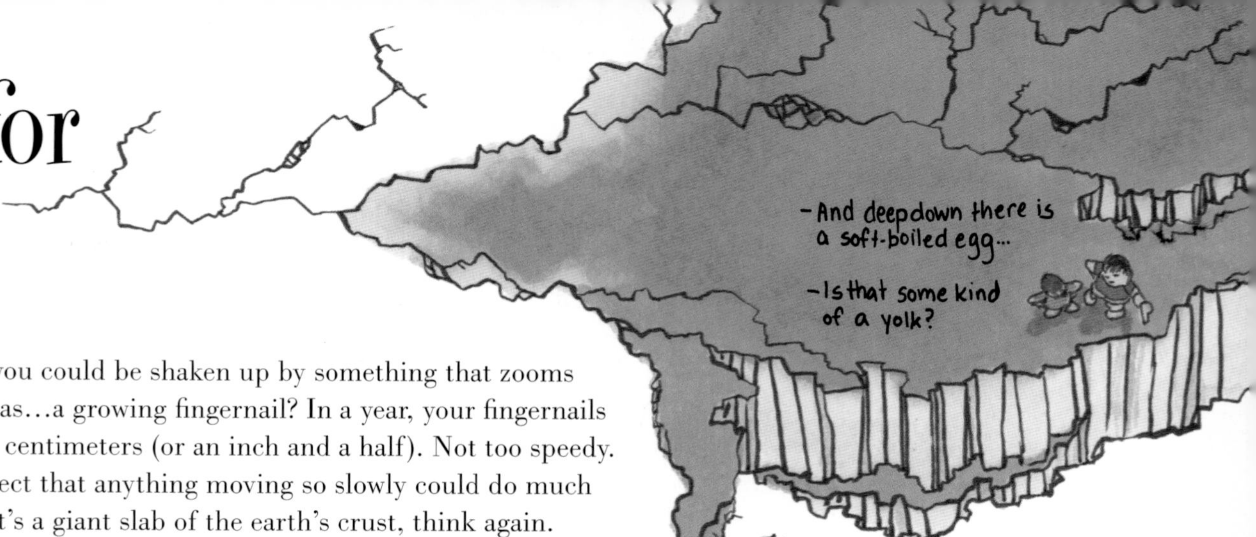

—And deep down there is a soft-boiled egg…

—Is that some kind of a yolk?

Do you think you could be shaken up by something that zooms along as fast as…a growing fingernail? In a year, your fingernails grow about 3 or 4 centimeters (or an inch and a half). Not too speedy. You wouldn't expect that anything moving so slowly could do much harm. But when it's a giant slab of the earth's crust, think again.

You can think of the surface of the earth as a cracked eggshell on a soft-boiled egg. The pieces of shell are continent-sized pieces of earth and rock called *tectonic plates*. Instead of goopy egg, the plates float on a layer of thick molten rock called the *mantle*. The mantle moves up, down, and around in currents. Because the plates are floating on top of it, they move with it, at a speed roughly equal to that of your fingernail's growth. Well, that's how fast they would move if they glided along at a steady speed. But they don't.

The place where colliding plates rub against each other is called a *fault*. Several things can happen at faults. One plate can duck under the other. Or one can smash head-on into the other, causing both to break and lift. Sometimes the edges of the plates slide along each other, moving in opposite directions. But gigantic slabs of jagged rock do not slide smoothly. Often they get stuck, and tremendous stress builds up along the fault. (And you thought you were under stress to get your homework done!) Eventually, after years of stress, the rocks along the plate boundaries suddenly jerk loose from each other. There's a name for that:

EARTHQUAKE!!!!

Believe it or not, this happens about a million times a year. On average, there is an earthquake once every 30 seconds. Fortunately, most of them are very small. But each year, about 8 to 10 of those quakes do significant damage—toppling buildings, snapping bridges in half, destroying highways, and killing or injuring those unlucky people in the wrong place at the wrong time.

In California, the San Andreas Fault has been the source of many earthquakes. It marks the meeting place of two enormous plates, the Pacific Plate and the North American Plate. The most famous quake took place at about 5 A.M. on April 18, 1906. Called the Great San Francisco Earthquake, it was one of the most violent and destructive quakes in United States history. Buildings crumbled to the ground and others—28,000 in all—were destroyed by fires from ruptured gas pipes. Earthquakes of equal or greater intensity have devastated many other parts of the world. Fortunately, today's architects and engineers have learned to design structures that can shake in a quake—and stay up to await the next one.

Introducing QUAKO

Faster than a growing fingernail! Able to move tall buildings in a single shrug! More powerful than, well… EVERYTHING!

His motto: "It's ALL my fault!"

…and F is also for

fertilization

fluid

fluorescence

force

freeze

frequency

fungus

fusion

Your hand. Mom's cookies. GRAVITY at work?

A HeMan Wannabe on Jupiter

I used to be a 98-Pound Weakling!

A Sumo Wrestler on the Moon

I've NEVER been a 98-Pound ANYTHING!

G is for Gravity

Jump up. What happens? You fall down.
But why do you fall down? Gravity.

What's gravity?

Now that's something people have been wondering for centuries.

Gravity is the pull that objects have on each other. All objects pull other things toward them. Everyone likes a little company. You're probably not too shocked to learn that the Earth's gravity pulls things toward its center, but this may surprise you: Your gravity pulls the Earth toward your center! The force you exert upon the Earth is exactly the same as the force the Earth exerts upon you, but because the Earth is so much more massive than you (100,000,000,000,000,000,000,000 times more massive, if you must know), its gravity has a huge effect on you, while your gravity has such a tiny effect upon the Earth that it can't be noticed or measured. Jump up and you'll notice the Earth's gravity as it pulls you back down. At the same time, you are pulling the Earth *up* by an itsy-bitsy-teenie-weenie amount. How does it feel to know that you, yes YOU, exert a force upon the Earth?

Of course, the Earth's gravity acts upon more than just you. Just try lifting a sack of potatoes. Do you feel all that gravity acting on the sack? Lift just one potato and you feel its gravity also, but because the single potato is much less massive than the entire sack, it feels a lot less heavy.

No matter where you go, your mass will always be the same. If you have a mass of 42 kilograms standing on the Earth, you will also have a mass of 42 kilograms on the Moon, Jupiter, or the Sun (though we doubt you'd stand there for long). But weight is not the same as mass. Mass is how much "stuff," or matter, you have, but weight is the force pulling you down toward the center of whatever planet or star you happen to be standing on. It depends partly on your own mass, and partly on the gravitational force of the heavenly body you're on. If you've just landed on Jupiter, you're going to be in for a real surprise when you step on the scale. There's a lot more gravitational pull on enormous Jupiter than on tiny Earth, so you'll weigh a lot more—nearly two and a half times more—even though your mass has not changed at all. To lighten up, try the Moon! The Moon is a lot less massive than Earth, so its gravitational pull on you is a lot smaller. In fact, you'd weigh about one-sixth of your Earth weight on the Moon.

Throughout most of the world, people measure their weight in kilograms (see **S is for Système International**). Scientifically speaking, though, kilograms are used to measure mass, not weight. The correct unit for measuring weight in the metric system is the *newton* (named for Sir Isaac). Since most people don't spend much time visiting other planets, they can get away with using a measurement for mass and calling it weight. We're willing to bet that even Nobel Prize–winning physicists give their weight in kilograms, although we've never actually had the nerve to ask any.

In the United States, people weigh themselves in pounds, which is indeed a unit of weight. (In the U.S. system, mass is measured in—get this!—*slugs*. If you weigh 100 pounds here on Earth, you have a mass of about $3\frac{1}{8}$ slugs.)

No matter which unit you use, it's easy to figure out how much you would weigh on the Moon, on the Sun, or on any planet. Just look at the list below and multiply your Earth weight by the number given. Notice that if you're going to a place less massive than Earth, you'll be multiplying by a number less than 1, so there your weight will be less than it is on Earth. If you're going to a place more massive than Earth, you'll multiply by a number greater than 1, so there your weight will be more than it is on Earth.

Moon	.166
Mercury	.378
Venus	.907
Mars	.379
Saturn	.916
Jupiter	2.63
Uranus	.889
Neptune	1.125
Pluto	.067
Sun	270.7

Okay, so now you know something about gravity. But how does gravity work? Perhaps the most amazing thing about gravity is this: Even though scientists have studied it and measured it for hundreds of years, no one really knows how it works.

Perhaps you will be the one to figure it out.

What is the gravitational force of the earth on you?

It's really easy to FIGure it out in newtons. On Earth, mass in kilograms × 9.762 = weight in newtons

Psst! If you don't know your mass in kilograms, multiply your weight in pounds × 2.2. But shhhh... don't tell anyone we said so. See S is for SI.

On Neptune mass: 1 slug weight: 36 lbs.

On Pluto mass: 1 slug weight: 21 lbs.

On Uranus mass: 1 slug weight: 28 lbs.

On Saturn mass: 1 slug weight: 29 lbs.

...and G is also for

gamete

gamma ray

gas

gene

g-force

On the Sun mass: 1 slug weight: 8,662 lbs

On Mercury mass: 1 slug weight: 12 lbs.

On Venus mass: 1 slug weight: 29 lbs.

On Earth mass: 1 slug weight: 32 lbs.

On Mars mass: 1 slug weight: 12 lbs.

On Jupiter mass: 1 slug weight: 84 lbs.

LIQUIDS

Me?

SOLIDS

more accurate than flattering

The Mouse Molecule

H_2O

Look familiar?

H is for H_2O

You probably know that H_2O is water. But did you know that you are water? Well, not all of you, but about two-thirds. If anyone asks you to describe yourself, you could say something like "three buckets of solids and six buckets of water." You would be just about right! But you're not the only thing that has more water than anything else—over three-quarters of Earth's surface is covered with water. In a grand drama called "Life on Earth," water would be the star of the show. That's a pretty serious role for a little molecule that looks like Mickey Mouse.

Mickey Mouse? That brings us back to H_2O. Why H_2O? It's the chemist's way of saying two hydrogen atoms (*H* means "hydrogen") and one oxygen atom (*O* means "oxygen"). (See **A is for Atom.**) When two hydrogen atoms and one oxygen atom get together, they are attracted to each other. This attraction doesn't lead to dating, but to something even more exciting: water!

You know from reading **A is for Atom** that atoms are mostly open space. There's a dense nucleus made of protons and neutrons in the middle, surrounded by a cloud of tiny particles called electrons travelling in regions called shells. Remember, the first shell can hold only two electrons. Outside it is another shell that can hold eight electrons. An atom with shells that do not have the maximum number of electrons is not a happy atom. Of course atoms don't have emotions, but they do have an ability to fill their shells. Sometimes an atom just "robs" an electron from another atom. (That doesn't sound very polite, but it happens.) Other times, atoms will share electrons. (That sounds much nicer, doesn't it?) Here's what happens with hydrogen and oxygen.

Hydrogen has only one electron. Since that one electron zooms around in a shell that can hold two, hydrogen is looking for an electron to fill its one and only shell. Oxygen has eight electrons. Two are in its first shell and six in its second shell. But that second shell can hold eight, so it is two short of its capacity. It "wants" two more electrons. Where oh where could it find two electrons? From a hydrogen atom? Good thinking, but you're not there yet. It will have to get them from two hydrogen atoms! If two H atoms nudge up against a single oxygen, each of them can share their single electron with the oxygen. Both the oxygen and hydrogen atoms will be "happy" because their shells will be complete. When two hydrogen atoms share their electrons with an oxygen atom in this way, they don't just hang out in any old place near the oxygen. They position themselves at an angle, which makes them look suspiciously like Mickey Mouse ears.

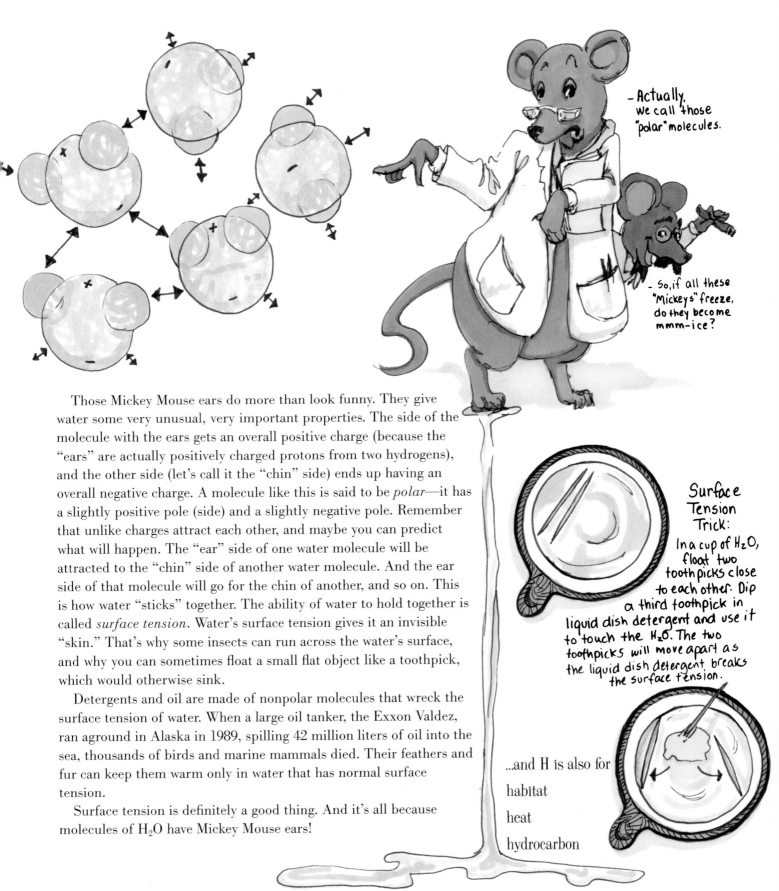

- Actually, we call those "polar" molecules.

- So, if all these "Mickeys" freeze, do they become mmm-ice?

Those Mickey Mouse ears do more than look funny. They give water some very unusual, very important properties. The side of the molecule with the ears gets an overall positive charge (because the "ears" are actually positively charged protons from two hydrogens), and the other side (let's call it the "chin" side) ends up having an overall negative charge. A molecule like this is said to be *polar*—it has a slightly positive pole (side) and a slightly negative pole. Remember that unlike charges attract each other, and maybe you can predict what will happen. The "ear" side of one water molecule will be attracted to the "chin" side of another water molecule. And the ear side of that molecule will go for the chin of another, and so on. This is how water "sticks" together. The ability of water to hold together is called *surface tension*. Water's surface tension gives it an invisible "skin." That's why some insects can run across the water's surface, and why you can sometimes float a small flat object like a toothpick, which would otherwise sink.

Detergents and oil are made of nonpolar molecules that wreck the surface tension of water. When a large oil tanker, the Exxon Valdez, ran aground in Alaska in 1989, spilling 42 million liters of oil into the sea, thousands of birds and marine mammals died. Their feathers and fur can keep them warm only in water that has normal surface tension.

Surface tension is definitely a good thing. And it's all because molecules of H_2O have Mickey Mouse ears!

Surface Tension Trick:
In a cup of H_2O, float two toothpicks close to each other. Dip a third toothpick in liquid dish detergent and use it to touch the H_2O. The two toothpicks will move apart as the liquid dish detergent breaks the surface tension.

...and H is also for

habitat

heat

hydrocarbon

SKUNK: NOT immune to cars

This illustration unavailable due to graphic nature of subject matter.

Worse than a dead skunk: your big brother's tennis shoes.

Your Immune System: Ready to attack 24/7

I is for Immune System

Ready for something gross? If not, skip the next paragraph. (We bet you won't!)

Think of a dead skunk lying on the ground. Let it sit there for a few warm days and what do you find? Flies buzzing around its eyes, worms exploring its head, bacteria and fungi feasting on its flesh, microbes and parasites of all kinds partying and multiplying like crazy. Come back a few weeks later and what do you find? Not much other than a skeleton. Everything else has been broken down, eaten up, or carted off. (See **R is for Rot.**)

So why isn't that happening to you now? Because living animals (including you) are protected by an amazing army of defenders that battle bacteria, viruses, microbes, parasites, and other microscopic invaders that would love to make a meal of your body. They do this every second of every minute of every hour of every day of your life. They are your true heroes. All together, they are known as your *immune system*. Without them you'd be a sorry sight—and an even sorrier smell!

Your immune system does more than keep you from looking and smelling like a dead skunk. It keeps you healthy. Every day you breathe in germs (viruses and bacteria) that could make you sick. Other germs enter your body through cuts in your skin. If you eat food with microbes or toxins on it, saliva and the acid in your stomach will kill most of them, but others may make it farther inside your body. What happens then? Most of the time, your immune system goes on the offensive. But it can get overwhelmed. It may take a week to mount a full-blown attack on a cold virus infection, and in the meantime, you're blowing your nose and feeling lousy. If bacteria get in through a cut, they may give you a skin infection before the clean-up squad can do their work of killing bacteria and mopping them up. Eat something nasty, and you can be laid low by food poisoning before your immune system wipes out the bad guys. If you are healthy, your immune system will eventually catch up with the germs, and you'll get better. People with AIDS have an immune system that doesn't work right, and when they get a cold, it can be very serious.

So just what is this immune system we're talking about? It's not a single organ, like your heart or brain. It's a whole menu of organs and tissues and cells and molecules that includes:

- Your skin, which helps keep the bad stuff out and also kills bacteria and mold that land on it (this is why you don't wake up looking green).
- Your spleen, an organ which filters your blood, looking for foreign cells.
- Your thymus, an organ where important disease-fighting white blood cells are readied for action.
- Your bone marrow, which makes red and white blood cells.
- Your lymph, a clearish liquid that bathes all your cells and drains away waste products. Lymph is filtered in lymph nodes to remove unwelcome bacteria. When lots of bacteria are being filtered out, your lymph nodes swell up, which is why your mother checks for swollen lymph nodes in your neck to see whether you're really sick or you just want to stay home.
- *Antibodies,* which are protein molecules made by white blood cells. They do such an important job that we're going to stop writing this list and meet you in the next paragraph to tell you about them. There are lots of other parts of the immune system we could list here, but we're going to cut it short because we have 17 more letters left to do—and besides, what do you think this is, a medical textbook?

About those antibodies: *anti-* means "against" and you know what *body* means, except in this case it doesn't mean your own body but the body of the germ that's invading you. When these germs are inside your body, we call them *antigens.* Antibodies fight antigens, not by punching them out, but by disabling them in a clever way. Most antibodies are made of four large protein molecules bonded together in the shape of a Y. Near the end of the Y is a special section that fits snugly over the shape of the particular antigen the antibody is attacking.

When an antibody binds to an antigen, it can stop it from invading cells or prevent it from giving off nasty chemicals. The antibody also signals to white blood cells that the intruder needs to be killed and carted off. Antibodies work only on the particular antigen they were designed for, so you need many thousands of different antibodies in your body to protect you against many kinds of invaders.

You have probably had vaccinations to immunize you against diseases like polio and diphtheria and whooping cough. What's really happening is that you're getting disease antigens that have been weakened so they can't hurt you. Your body doesn't realize they are harmless, so it still makes the antibodies that would disable them if they were the real thing. Later, if the genuine germs come along, the cells that made those antibodies are ready and waiting. They quickly make new antibodies to fight the germs before they can multiply and make you seriously ill. The vaccine has tricked your immune system into doing something really helpful.

Unfortunately, this trick can work both ways. Sometimes your

An immune system at work

1. Your little brother grabs his sick pal's toy. It's REALLY germy.

2. He sticks his germy finger in his nose.

Helloooo, antigens!

3. The antigens INVADE.

Yeehaw! Fresh cells! (microscopic view)

BUT this alerts his immune system...

4. So, made-to-match antibodies nab the nasty antigens.

Ulp!

Your little brother gets well, and you get to babysit again.

The Good News!
Hooray!

A vaccine

made of weakened antigens

triggers new antibodies that stay to protect you from

Strong antigens that could make you REALLY sick.

The Bad News
Boo! *Hiss!*

A harmless pollen

is mistaken as bad by antibodies.

Your immune system goes into attack mode

and you feel ROTTEN.

immune system does things we wish it wouldn't do. It can launch into attack mode to destroy things that aren't really harmful. For example, when pollen lands on your eyes and gets sucked into your nose and throat, the immune system triggers your nose to run and your eyes to tear because that helps flush out the antigens even though they are harmless. Some people have immune systems that actually attack parts of their own bodies. This is sad but true. Rheumatoid arthritis is a terrible disease in which people's immune systems destroy their joints so badly that they may be unable to walk or move their fingers. Talk about inappropriate behavior! Medical researchers are trying to find ways to get the immune system to work when we want it to, and chill out when we don't.

But for most people most of the time, the immune system does an amazing job. What we've told you here is only a small part of the story. Your immune system is incredibly complicated and it doesn't just ward off germs. It also helps repair cuts and broken bones, fights off big enemies like tapeworms and other parasites that want to live inside you, mops up dead and dying cells, and even clears up pimples! Without it, you'd be. . .well, you'd be dead.

Have you thanked your immune system today?

...and I is also for

inertia

infrared

inorganic

invertebrate

ionic bond

isotope

J is for Jet Propulsion

Blow up a balloon and squeeze the opening shut. Then let go. What happens? The balloon turns into a rocket. The same thing that propels rockets and jets is now propelling your balloon. It's called *jet propulsion*. Sir Isaac Newton didn't actually use the words "jet propulsion" in his laws of motion. Instead he said that a force applied in one direction gives rise to an equal force in the opposite direction. This is called *Newton's Third Law of Motion*. Sometimes people summarize it like this: Every action has an equal but opposite reaction. (If you tweak your little brother's ear, you will definitely get a reaction, but that's not the kind of action and reaction we're talking about.)

You have experienced Newton's Third Law of Motion if you've ever been on inline skates. You push backwards with one skate. That's the action. What happens? Your body slides forward. That's the reaction. You skate up to a wall and push your arms forward against the wall. Now your body goes backwards. If you mounted a large cannon on the deck of a ship and fired cannonballs off the back deck, the ship would be pushed forward. That would be a dangerous way to sail, so we definitely don't recommend it.

In a rocket, engines send exhaust streaming out the back end. That's the action. The reaction is the rocket taking off into the sky. Some people think a rocket works because the gases shooting out the back end are pushing against the air—like you pushing against the wall with your skates on. Good try, but it's not how a rocket works. In fact, a rocket works even better in space, where there's no air to push against, than it does near Earth. That's because in space the exhaust gases can rush out really fast without any air to slow them down. Since the gases are going backwards really fast, the rocket goes forward really fast. Jet planes work in more or less the same way, by burning fuel and shooting the exhaust backwards to propel the plane forward.

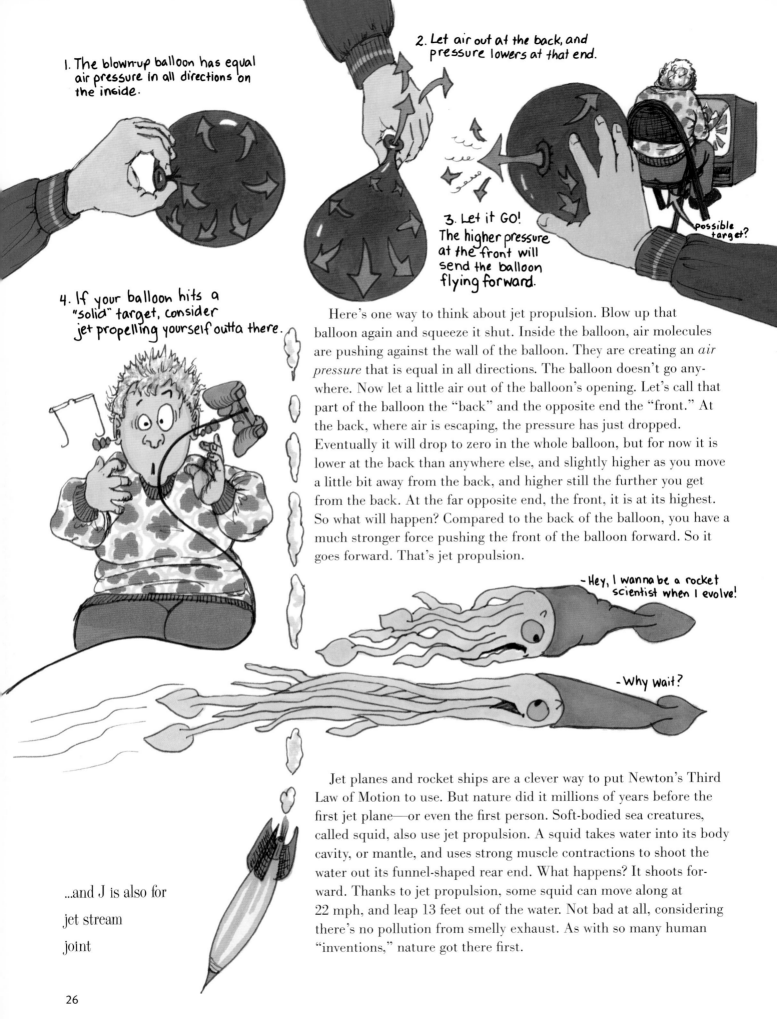

1. The blown-up balloon has equal air pressure in all directions on the inside.

2. Let air out at the back, and pressure lowers at that end.

3. Let it GO! The higher pressure at the front will send the balloon flying forward.

possible target?

4. If your balloon hits a "solid" target, consider jet propelling yourself outta there.

Here's one way to think about jet propulsion. Blow up that balloon again and squeeze it shut. Inside the balloon, air molecules are pushing against the wall of the balloon. They are creating an *air pressure* that is equal in all directions. The balloon doesn't go anywhere. Now let a little air out of the balloon's opening. Let's call that part of the balloon the "back" and the opposite end the "front." At the back, where air is escaping, the pressure has just dropped. Eventually it will drop to zero in the whole balloon, but for now it is lower at the back than anywhere else, and slightly higher as you move a little bit away from the back, and higher still the further you get from the back. At the far opposite end, the front, it is at its highest. So what will happen? Compared to the back of the balloon, you have a much stronger force pushing the front of the balloon forward. So it goes forward. That's jet propulsion.

– Hey, I wanna be a rocket scientist when I evolve!

– Why wait?

Jet planes and rocket ships are a clever way to put Newton's Third Law of Motion to use. But nature did it millions of years before the first jet plane—or even the first person. Soft-bodied sea creatures, called squid, also use jet propulsion. A squid takes water into its body cavity, or mantle, and uses strong muscle contractions to shoot the water out its funnel-shaped rear end. What happens? It shoots forward. Thanks to jet propulsion, some squid can move along at 22 mph, and leap 13 feet out of the water. Not bad at all, considering there's no pollution from smelly exhaust. As with so many human "inventions," nature got there first.

...and J is also for

jet stream

joint

K is for Kitchen

Sample Supervisor:
Grandma
Always ready for anything.
Probably a former stunt double.
(you never know)

"Kitchen" may not be a scientific term, but it's a great place to do science. Your kitchen is really a laboratory. It has countertops to work on, a stove (or microwave, or both) to heat things, a refrigerator and freezer to cool them, instruments for measuring ingredients, and—we hope—a fire extinguisher just in case you mess up big time! You can do so many science experiments in your kitchen that you might wonder why scientists bother driving in traffic to get to a lab (where it's much harder to make chocolate chip cookies!).

So what kind of science can you learn about in the kitchen? How about biology, chemistry, and physics? If that isn't enough, you can also learn about some aspects of geology—and maybe meteorology, too. And, perhaps most importantly, you can learn about how scientists conduct experiments. We could fill this whole book with kitchen science, but we are going to limit ourselves to just one tasty chemistry experiment. Normally you aren't supposed to eat anything you make in a science lab, but today we'll make an exception.

Here's a message from our lawyer (we believe it, too): *You should do this experiment ONLY with adult supervision. You will be using a stove, so you absolutely MUST get permission. And be EXTREMELY careful because you'll be working with a liquid hotter than boiling water.* That applies to everything we suggest you do. If you're not sure how to do something, ask an adult who does. Okay, now let's begin.

Winning the
NOBEL PRIZE
might start
here!

27

-Im supersaturated with homework.
-I have just the solution.
-How sweet!

A solute...

A solvent...

(Is this glass half empty or half full? Oh, whoops! Wrong book!)

and, finally...

A SOLUTION!

Let's keep stirring things up....

Stir some sugar into a glass of warm water—just a little at first.

When you can't see any more sugar in the glass, you have a sugar *solution*. A solution is a mixture in which individual molecules of something (the *solute*) are dissolved, or mixed evenly, in a liquid (the *solvent*). In this solution, the solute is the sugar and the solvent is the water. To prove to yourself that the sugar molecules are mixed evenly in the water, you can use a straw to taste some of the solution from the top, middle, and bottom of the glass. All your samples should taste equally sweet.

Keep adding sugar until no more of it will dissolve.

The solution is now *saturated*, meaning it is full and can hold no more. Can you think of a way to get even more sugar to dissolve? You might want to try some magical incantations, but we suggest you simply heat the solution.

Pour everything into a pot (make sure to scrape out any undissolved sugar) and put it over a burner at a low setting.

The sugar will start to dissolve. Slowly add more sugar until again it refuses to dissolve. Once again you have a saturated solution. The higher the temperature of a solution, the more sugar you can add before the solution becomes saturated. If you want to sound like a high-falutin' scientist, you could say, "Sugar solubility is proportional to water temperature," which is a fancy way of saying what we said in the sentence just before. You might also say that the intensity of smells coming out of the kitchen is proportional to the intensity of shouts coming from the nearest adult.

If you're feeling experimental, you could try to answer another question: Do all things dissolve in the same way? Are some things more soluble (meaning more willing to dissolve) than others? Since we already saw that temperature has a big influence on how much a substance will dissolve, you will want to use a thermometer and try to keep the temperature the same as you test different solutes to see if they all dissolve in the same way. You can try dissolving table salt, epsom salts, and baking soda, to name a few.

Here's another question: Do solutions freeze at a higher temperature or a lower temperature or the same temperature as pure water? Can you design an experiment to answer the question? We suggest you try it with salt solutions. Once you get some answers, you may be able to explain why highway workers sometimes put salt on roads in freezing weather, and why ship captains prefer seaports to freshwater ports in cold climates. If you can design and carry out an experiment that answers this question, CONGRATULATIONS! You have just done "real science." Real science means discovering something for yourself through observation and experimentation—not by just looking it up. Real scientists are in the business of discovering new things that can't be looked up.

Back to your hot sugar solution, also known as syrup (another one of those highly scientific terms). If you let it cool back to room temperature, the solvent (water) will still hold more solute (sugar)

Ingredients:
1 willing adult
1 c. sugar
½ c. H₂O
clean jelly jar
string
pencil or wire
swizzle sticks, or
small weight on a string

and

patience

1. Boil the sugar and water 1 minute.

2. Pour into a clean jelly jar.

3. Suspend weighted string from a pencil, stick or wire—or just lean swizzle sticks against side of jar.

4. Remove surface crystals daily.

than it normally would at that temperature. A solution like that is *supersaturated*. Let's make one.

Slowly heat a cup of sugar in half a cup of water. Use a low flame, so it doesn't burn.

Once the sugar is dissolved, let it boil for a minute, again being careful not to burn it (unless you like to wash pots). Let it cool.

You have made a supersaturated solution. There is a nifty (and yummy) way to get that sugar out of solution and back into its solid state. *Here's where you have to be especially careful. Get an adult to help you with this part.*

Pour the syrup into a clean jelly jar. Suspend the swizzle sticks with string from a stick or piece of wire placed across the top of the jar. Or, just drop them in the jar, leaning them against the side. If you don't have a swizzle stick, a string tied to a small weight, like a clean metal washer, works well, too.

Leave the open jar undisturbed at room temperature, and don't move the swizzle sticks at all.

Check the jar every day. Within a few days the dissolved sugar will start to come out of solution and form crystals on the swizzle sticks. You'll probably find some on the surface too. Gently remove surface crystals so the solution can continue to evaporate.

Large crystals take a week or more to grow, so be patient.

Before you pig out on sweet swizzle sticks, take a close look at the crystals you have grown. Use a magnifying glass, and compare them with crystals of granulated sugar. Are they the same shape? Compare the shape of sugar crystals with salt crystals. A crystal's shape reflects the shape of its atoms or molecules and how they fit together. Chemists learn a great deal from studying crystals, and you can, too—right in your own kitchen!

Okay, now that you're finished with your chemistry experiment, eat it.

Okay, sometimes I DO eat homework!

...and K is also for

Kelvin

keratin

kinetic energy

kingdom

white
light

equilateral prism

L is for Light

Sir Isaac Newton thought light was made of particles.

Hmmm... I think I'll use these particles of red paint to represent the particles of red light reflected from the cherries.

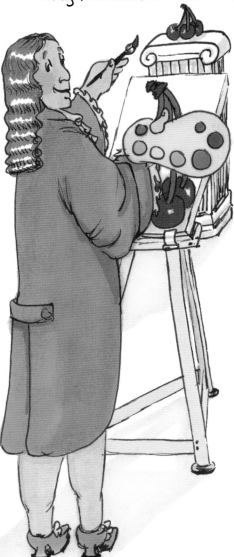

Light is strange stuff. How strange? Well, scientists aren't even sure it's stuff at all. Sometimes light acts like it's made up of *particles*, or tiny bits of stuff; other times it acts like a *wave* of energy. Waves or particles, particles or waves? After years of head scratching, scientists finally decided that light has a split personality, showing properties of both waves and particles.

Scientists love to measure things, so you can look in almost any physics textbook and find out that waves of visible light are longer than waves of X rays but shorter than microwaves. Just in case you're wondering what the *wavelength* of light is, we'll tell you that it can be anywhere between roughly 400 and 700 nanometers (nm), which means 400 to 700 billionths of a meter.

So you're not impressed. You're saying, "Who cares if it's 400 nm or 700 nm or something in between?" We'll tell you who cares. You do. The difference between 400 nm and 700 nm is like the difference between blue and red. Actually, it *is* the difference between blue and red. The exact wavelength of light is what gives it color. If light came only in one wavelength—say 550 nm—everything you saw would be just one color. Your life would be as dull as if you were stuck inside a black-and-white TV. (Actually, it would be a green-and-white TV because 550 nm is the wavelength of green.)

People usually think of color as a part of whatever they're looking at. The cherry is red, the bird is blue, your face is looking a little green, and so forth. But scientists have known otherwise since 1666. That's when Sir Isaac Newton met a colorful character named Roy G. Biv. Well, what actually happened was that Newton held up a three-sided piece of glass called a *prism*, shined a beam of light through it, and watched the light fan out to become all the colors of the rainbow. The colorful band of light, called a *spectrum*, had red on top, orange beneath it, then yellow, green, blue, and violet.

Newton figured out that white light contains all of these colors, and when the prism bent the light rays, it separated them. Now we know that the different wavelengths of light appear to us as different colors. Red has the longest wavelength, violet has the shortest, and all the other colors are somewhere in between. In white light, the many colors are mixed together, but when they pass through the prism, they start to show their true colors, so to speak. The longer waves pass more easily through the prism while the shorter waves bend more,

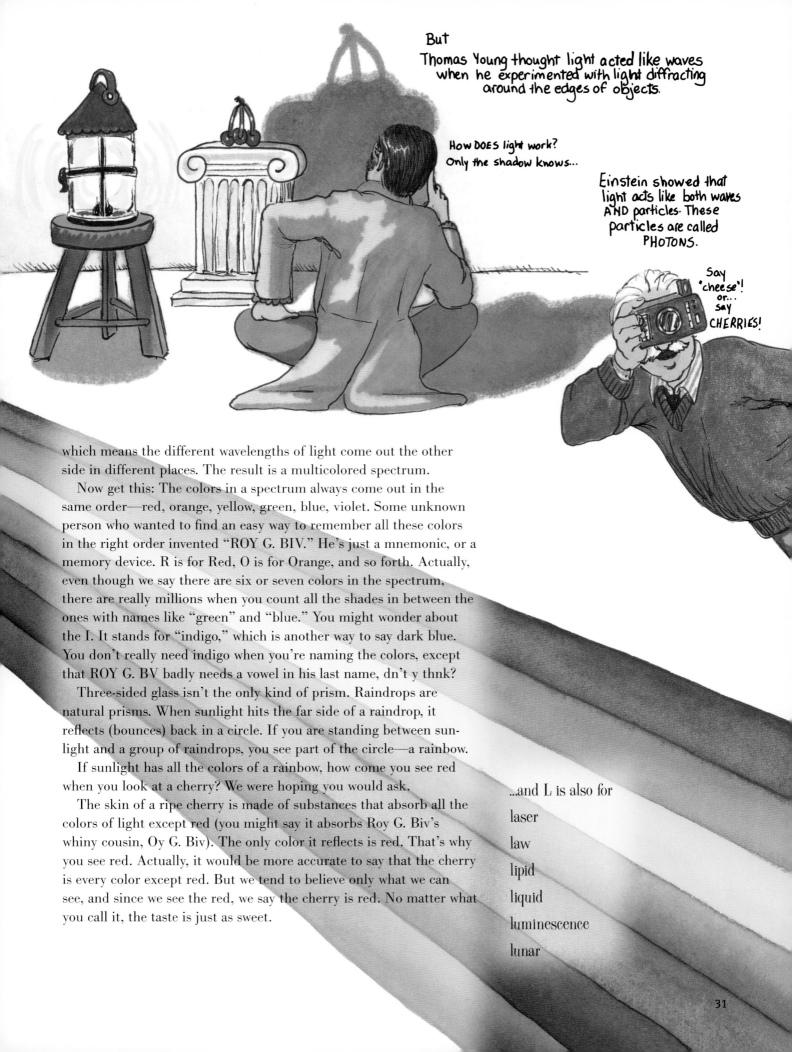

But Thomas Young thought light acted like waves when he experimented with light diffracting around the edges of objects.

How DOES light work? Only the shadow knows...

Einstein showed that light acts like both waves AND particles. These particles are called PHOTONS.

Say "cheese"! or... say CHERRIES!

which means the different wavelengths of light come out the other side in different places. The result is a multicolored spectrum.

Now get this: The colors in a spectrum always come out in the same order—red, orange, yellow, green, blue, violet. Some unknown person who wanted to find an easy way to remember all these colors in the right order invented "ROY G. BIV." He's just a mnemonic, or a memory device. R is for Red, O is for Orange, and so forth. Actually, even though we say there are six or seven colors in the spectrum, there are really millions when you count all the shades in between the ones with names like "green" and "blue." You might wonder about the I. It stands for "indigo," which is another way to say dark blue. You don't really need indigo when you're naming the colors, except that ROY G. BV badly needs a vowel in his last name, dn't y thnk?

Three-sided glass isn't the only kind of prism. Raindrops are natural prisms. When sunlight hits the far side of a raindrop, it reflects (bounces) back in a circle. If you are standing between sunlight and a group of raindrops, you see part of the circle—a rainbow.

If sunlight has all the colors of a rainbow, how come you see red when you look at a cherry? We were hoping you would ask.

The skin of a ripe cherry is made of substances that absorb all the colors of light except red (you might say it absorbs Roy G. Biv's whiny cousin, Oy G. Biv). The only color it reflects is red. That's why you see red. Actually, it would be more accurate to say that the cherry is every color except red. But we tend to believe only what we can see, and since we see the red, we say the cherry is red. No matter what you call it, the taste is just as sweet.

...and L is also for

laser

law

lipid

liquid

luminescence

lunar

31

M is for Music

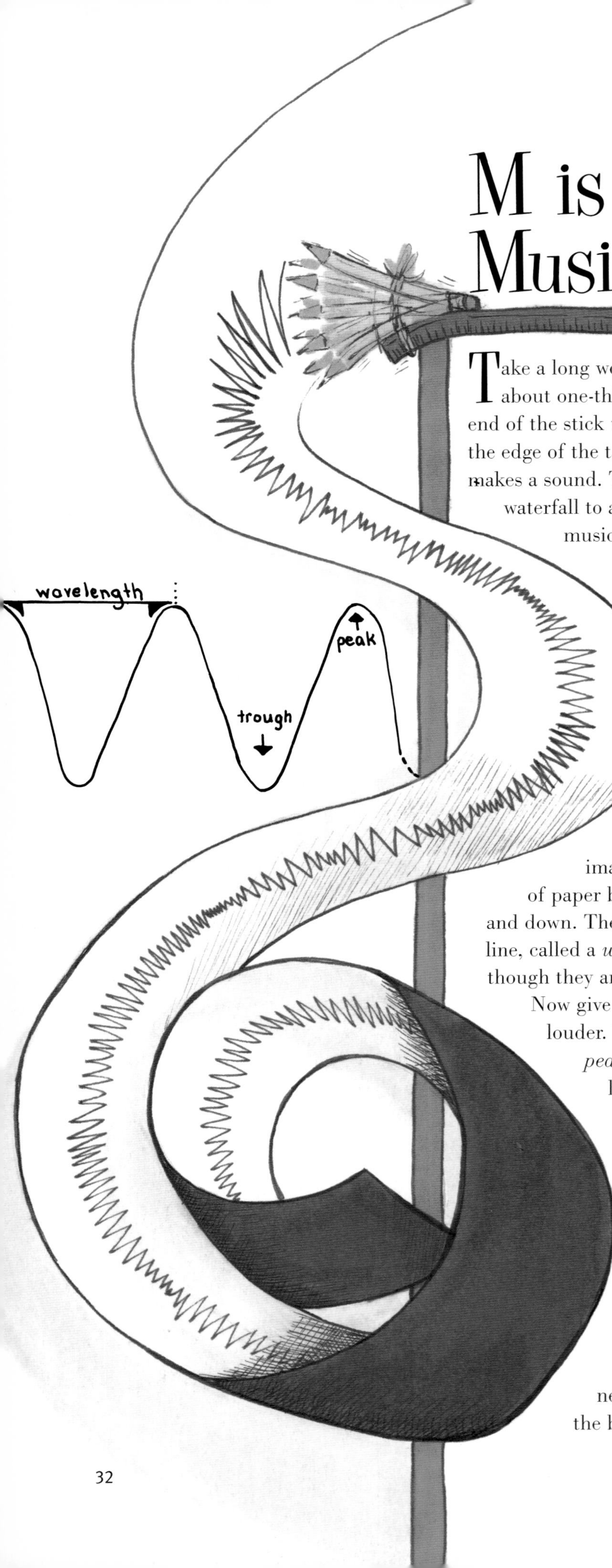

Take a long wooden ruler and place it on the edge of a table so that about one-third hangs off. Give a pretty good whomp to the free end of the stick with one hand while pressing the other end firmly to the edge of the table (don't let go!). The stick starts to vibrate. It makes a sound. That's what sound is: *vibration*. From a thunderous waterfall to a gentle lullaby, all sound is vibration. (We'll get to music in a minute.)

Vibrations push nearby air molecules together (as the object moves towards them) and then pull them apart (as the object moves away from them). These waves of bunched-together molecules and spread-out molecules move away from the vibrating thing in every direction, the same way circular waves spread away from a pebble thrown into a still lake. The waves caused by vibration are called *sound waves*.

While the ruler is *thwonking* away, you might imagine a pencil stuck to the end of it, and a long sheet of paper being pulled past the pencil as the ruler vibrates up and down. The pencil would make a wavy line on the paper. That line, called a *waveform*, would let you "see" sound waves even though they are invisible.

Now give that ruler a really good *thunk*. The sound gets louder. What happens to the waveform? Its high points, or *peaks*, get higher and its low points, or *troughs*, get lower. Next, gently *tweak* the ruler to make a softer sound. What happens to the line? The peaks and troughs are smaller.

The loudness or softness of a sound is called its "volume." Musicians describe volume with Italian words like *piano* and *pianissimo* (for soft and very soft) or *forte* and *fortissimo* (for loud and very loud). Scientists think about the volume of sound in a slightly different way. They look at its waveform to see how bumpy it is—that is, how high its peaks are. Instead of describing the loudness with words, scientists measure the height of the bumps.

wavelength

peak

trough

Let's do one other thing with that ruler. Slide it in a little bit so a shorter section is sticking out over the edge of the table, and then *thwonk* the free end again. Do you notice that the sound is higher? What do you see when you look at the vibrating part of the ruler? It's moving faster, right? If you were still drawing an imaginary line with an imaginary pencil on imaginary moving paper, you would notice that the peaks are now closer together. As a sound gets higher, musicians say its "pitch" goes up, but scientists say it has a *higher frequency*, which means more "vibrations per second." The note that musicians call "middle A" has a frequency of 440 vibrations per second. Higher notes will have more vibrations per second and lower notes will have fewer. On a waveform, peaks will be closer to each other (and so will troughs) for higher sounds and further apart for lower sounds.

Suppose you played the note A on a piano, and then went up eight white keys to another A. A musician would say the second A is one "octave" higher than the first A. What would a scientist say? If she loves music and plays an instrument, as many scientists do, she might say it's gone up one octave! But a scientist would also say that the frequency has doubled. Now, instead of vibrating 440 times per second, the sound is vibrating 880 times per second. If you drew out the waveform showing an entire second of vibrations, it would have 880 peaks and 880 troughs.

The strings of a violin behave a lot like the ruler hanging out over your table. A violinist changes the length of the violin's strings when he presses them against the fingerboard. Well, he doesn't exactly change the length of the string, but he changes the length of the part that can vibrate. The shorter the vibrating part, the more vibrations per second—and the higher the pitch.

But string instruments have more than one string. Some strings are thicker than others. A thicker string vibrates more slowly than a thinner one, so it has a lower pitch. In some instruments, like the piano, there is no way to change the length of the string. Instead, these instruments have many different strings—some short and thin, some long and thick, and lots in between. Each has its own pitch.

A wind instrument is basically a hollow tube with a mouthpiece. The player blows into the mouthpiece, which causes something to vibrate—in woodwinds, a wooden reed vibrates, and in brass instruments the lips of the musician give off the vibrations. Either way, these vibrations really shake up the air inside the instrument, and it starts vibrating too. When you think about it, this

It's a String Thing!

1. High notes are made by plucking a short or thin string.

2. Low notes are made by plucking a long or thick string.

3. Soft notes are made by gently strumming any string.

4. Loud notes are made by really THWONKING that string.

5. How are beautiful notes made? By tying all the strings together and whomping away... KNOT!

6. And Grandma's day is made when you share these notes with her. Go on—give her some good vibrations!

How some musicians get their start...
(and some get their finish).

...and M is also for

mammal

meiosis

melt

mineral

mitosis

molecule

momentum

moon

isn't so different from a violin or cello string, except that it's a column of air that's vibrating. The wind player has a way of making the vibrating air column longer or shorter. In a flute, he puts fingers down over certain holes. Only the air under the closed holes can vibrate. In a trumpet, she opens and closes valves, which routes the air through shorter or longer paths. Longer paths mean lower pitch and shorter paths mean higher pitch. (Trombones have a nifty way of lengthening the air column, which you will quickly learn if you ever come too close to one when its player reaches for a low note.)

A vibrating string or air column, all by itself, would be very hard to hear. So every musical instrument has a body that increases its volume and gives it the particular qualities that makes a violin sound so different from a trumpet or a bassoon. Ask a music teacher to lend you a tuning fork and show you how to get it vibrating. Listen to it. You will hear a tone, but it won't be very loud. You may have to hold the fork close to your ear to hear it at all. Strike it again and quickly set the base of the tuning fork on a wooden tabletop. It gets louder, doesn't it? That's because the vibrations go from the fork to the table, which vibrates with a lot more volume than the fork itself. Try putting it on different surfaces (not fine furniture, please!). Do you hear the same note? It should have the same pitch, but, depending on where you put it, a different volume and sound quality.

Now wash the fork to make sure it's clean enough to put in your mouth. That's what you're going to do. No, don't swallow it—your music teacher wouldn't like that and neither would your doctor!—but put the vibrating fork against your front teeth. Why do you think the sound gets louder? Because the fork is making the bones inside your head vibrate! Now make some funny faces by opening and closing your mouth and throat in different ways while the fork is vibrating. Listen to the changes in sound quality. You are making different parts of your head vibrate in different ways, and there is a difference in the sound produced. When you talk or sing, the vocal cords in your larynx produce vibrations, and the different parts of your head, throat, and chest work like the body of a musical instrument. Everyone's body is different, so everyone's voice is different. (Men usually have longer, thicker vocal cords than women, which is why their voices tend to be lower in pitch.)

Of course there's a lot more to music than understanding the sounds produced by instruments. Music is an art form. It is an expression of emotions. No one can say whether it's beautiful (or awful) except the person listening. Not everything can be boiled down to pure science. We think that's a good thing. Most scientists and music lovers would probably agree.

N is for
Natural Selection

Vegetable Ancestors
that someone must've selected

Very Old Carrot
(always rooted for the bad guys)

Ancient Corn
(probably used to stalk other vegetables)

Aw shucks! Howdja guess?

And you thought it was hard to eat them TODAY!

What? I fetched it, didn't I?

Let's say you want to create a new breed of dog. Your dogs will have a curly tail and a colored patch over their right eye. And, since you're lazy in the morning, they must be good at learning to fetch newspapers. So, to start your breed, you look over all the dogs at the local shelter. When you find a male with an eye patch and a female with a curly tail, you take them home, and hope they will get along famously. A few months later, the female gives birth to a litter of nine pups. Only two have both eye patches and curly tails, so you keep them and give the others away. When the two keepers are old enough, you start training them to fetch the paper.

Several months later, one of your growing pups has "got it": She brings you the paper every morning.

While you're waiting for the female to grow up, you start looking for a male. Finally, you find one who seems intelligent and has an eye patch though no curly tail. You breed him with your female, and from their litter of pups, you are delighted to find one who has both an eye patch and a curly tail. A little training and he's got the newspaper trick, too.

And so it goes, through the doggie generations. You keep looking for pups with the traits you like, and when they are old enough, you breed them with other dogs that have similar traits until you have a yard full of dogs, all of whom have those three traits. You have created a new breed.

This process is called *artificial selection*. It is "artificial" because it has been done by people, not by nature, and it is "selection" because only certain dogs were chosen, or "selected," to be parents of the next generation. They were selected because they possess the traits you like (curly tail, eye patch, and the ability to learn tricks). These traits are defined in the DNA of the dog's genes (see **D is for DNA**) and they may be passed on to the next generation.

Animal and plant breeders have been doing this sort of thing for thousands of years. The crops we eat and the domesticated animals we raise were changed by artificial selection over many generations. You probably wouldn't want to eat the wild ancestors of carrots or corn, and you wouldn't want the wild ancestor of dogs or cats in your house!

In the 19th century, an English naturalist named Charles Darwin realized that nature can also do the job of deciding which parents get to pass their traits on to another generation. In fact, nature has been doing it for a lot longer than people have been around.

For a full comprehension of NATURAL SELECTION, start here:

Scene 1 — The Desert Island (Bummer!)

slow munchker: monster meal

uhoh

hungry monster

Scene 2

Oh, those caves are lookin' good...

not-so-fast munchker

much faster munchker

RIP

BURP! Ahhh...zzzzz

Scene 3 — Rats! All the slow munchkers are gone. Now what do the monsters do, since it's no longer a "dessert" island?

Solution! As time passes, monsters evolve longer arms.

This little piggy...

Somehow, I don't think I'll make a good parent...

Imagine an island with two kinds of creatures: monsters and munchkers. The monsters are big and hungry. The munchkers are small and tasty. The island has no trees, but it has many caves where munchkers can hide from pursuing monsters.

Along comes a monster. All the munchkers scatter into a nearby cave. The fast munchkers make it safely inside, but pity the ones who are just a little too slow. You know what happens to them: chomp, chomp, chomp. Delicious! Those munchkers are now monster food.

Of course dead munchkers do not make good parents. Their genes die with them, and their traits do not get passed on to the next generation. Instead, the fleet-footed munchkers who escaped the monsters are much more likely to live long enough to reproduce and pass their genes on to another generation—including the genes that affect quickness. So, over time, there will be more fast munchkers and fewer slow ones. Some people call this "survival of the fittest." Fast munchkers are "fitter" than slow ones because they are better able to escape danger. Their genes will be the ones that tend to "survive" through the generations. The scientific name for this process is *natural selection*.

Natural selection also works on the monsters. Maybe a few of them have long arms and flexible shoulders that let them reach a long way into the cave openings to yank out cowering munchkers. Over time, more and more of the monsters will become long-armed because long-armed monsters are more likely to eat well and live to reproduce. Eventually, all the monsters may have long arms.

It's hard to predict how natural selection will work. It works differently in different places. Another way to say this is that natural selection depends on the environment. For instance, suppose some munchkers and monsters live on another island with tall trees but no caves. Here we might expect the munchkers to develop a climbing ability. But monsters might also get good at climbing trees (in pursuit of the munchkers). Then, perhaps munchkers would develop another defense. Perhaps those with smelly armpits would be the ones to survive because their odor is strong enough to knock pursuing monsters right out of the trees! The smelly ones would then live to pass along their genes for smelliness. Over many years, munchkers

Meanwhile, let's visit another island:

Scene 4 → Tropical Paradise (if you're a munchker)

Scene 5 →

But wait! What have we here?

If they won't use deodorant, maybe **I** can use this!

Sometimes, it's INTELLIGENCE that evolves...

would get smellier and smellier because the smelliest ones are the least likely to become monster food. But, of course, natural selection could also help monsters to develop ways of combatting bad smells. Maybe their noses would simply stop smelling the chemical found in munchker armpits.

These changes are part of the process of *evolution*. All species evolve gradually over time. If the animals (or plants) that are changing in one way and the animals (or plants) that are changing in another way do not have a chance to breed with each other, the two groups will eventually be so different that they can be considered separate kinds, or *species*. Think of the munchkers. Eventually, the tree-climbing smelly armpit type on one island and the fast-running cave-hiding type on the other island could become entirely different species.

We made up the monsters and munchkers, of course, but you can actually see evolution take place. You either have to live thousands of years, or you can use creatures that reproduce really fast, like bacteria. Even though individual bacteria are too small to see without a microscope, you can see colonies of them growing in special containers, called *petri dishes*, in the laboratory. If you add certain chemicals, called *antibiotics*, you will kill most of the bacteria in the dish. But a few will survive because they have genes that "resist" the antibiotic. Since the resistant bacteria are the only ones that survive to reproduce, they pass along the genes for resistance to their offspring. After a while, only resistant bacteria remain in the dish. For this strain of bacteria, the antibiotic is useless. This is not just a lab experiment! It happens to real bacteria that make real people sick. Really.

Of course most species evolve much more slowly than bacteria. It can take thousands of years for species to change in small ways, and millions of years for whole new groups of animals or plants to evolve. It has taken several billion years for primitive single-celled organisms oozing through the ancient mud to develop into the many complex creatures found all over Earth today. One particular species is so successful that it has time for leisure activities, like playing football. Without natural selection, those football players might still be flopping around in the mud. Come to think of it, maybe they still are.

Scene 6 →

What the...? I STILL smell armpits!

GENUINE MUNCHKER HIDE

Sometimes not.

...and N is also for

natural history

nerve

neuron

nucleus

Does your teacher shave with Occam's Razor?

An example:
Which excuse will he buy?

a. My homework? Well, this alien was selling lightbulbs in the woods where my sister's Girl Scout troup was camped too close to a volcano that erupted all over my paper so it's not ready... but... uh...

OR

b. My homework? I forgot it.

- Mmm! S'mores! They're almost as tasty as lightbulbs.

...and O is also for
orbit
organelles
organic
osmosis
ovary
ovum
ozone

O is for Occam's Razor

William of Occam was an English philosopher who invented shaving. No, just kidding. Occam developed a principle that has guided scientific thinking since the 13th century. What the principle says is very simple. In fact, it is about simplicity. It says that if you can choose between several explanations for something you have observed, the simplest one is probably right. The principle is called *Occam's razor* because by eliminating the complex explanations, you are "shaving" away all the nonsense.

Okay, let's do some shaving. Suppose you and your family are walking through the countryside one warm summer night and you are surprised to see an eerie orange glow emanating from woods near the base of some low hills. What is causing the orange glow? Together, you list some possibilities:

- An alien spaceship has landed and its parking lights are on.
- A group of lightbulb salespeople is holding a convention in the woods and they are demonstrating next year's models.
- One of the hills has just experienced a volcanic eruption and glowing hot lava is flowing down its side.
- The local Girl Scout troop is having a campfire and the girls are roasting marshmallows for s'mores.

So, which will it be? If you use Occam's razor you'll find three rather complicated ideas and one simple one.

Many folks believe UFOs are all over the place, but these people never seem to find any physical evidence. It's hard to explain aliens building a spaceship, finding Earth, landing safely, and departing without leaving any evidence behind. Lightbulb salespeople might have conventions—but in the woods? At night? How would they light up their wares? Volcanoes exist, but if you were near an active volcano, you'd probably know it. And besides, how could hot lava flow into a woodland and cause just an "eerie orange glow," not a giant firestorm?

On the other hand, a group of Girl Scouts around a campfire is easy to explain and easy to imagine. Occam's razor says to shave the first three away. The last one, the simplest one, is probably right. We'll betcha two s'mores and a mug of hot cocoa that the eerie glow is coming from a bunch of Girl Scouts.

Wait a minute! Do you hear that strange sound? It must be the spaceship taking off. . . or is it a campfire song?

P is for pH

PH? That's a pHunny looking word, isn't it? Well, it isn't really a word. It's an abbreviation for *potential Hydrogen*. But knowing what it stands for doesn't tell you much. And knowing its exact definition will tell you even less, but here it is: pH is the negative logarithm, to the base ten, of a solution's hydrogen ion concentration. Now you can impress your parents and your friends, but it probably won't mean much to them either. So now we'll explain pH in pLain English!

pH is a kind of measurement. Scientists measure lots of things, and when they're looking at a liquid, one of the things they may want to measure is its pH. That tells them if the liquid is *acidic* or *basic*, and how strong or weak it is. You've probably heard of acids. They're liquids that can burn the skin. (You've probably seen this in an old horror movie or two.) But many acids are perfectly edible, although they often taste sour. Lemon juice is sour and, sure enough, it has acids in it. Orange juice and grapefruit juice and vinegar also have acids. In fact, many foods are acidic.

You may not have heard of bases but you rub a base on your skin every day. (At least we hope you do.) Soap has a base in it, and so do detergents, bleach, ammonia, and other cleaning products. Most bases feel slippery, but be careful what you touch: A strong base can be as dangerous as a strong acid. There aren't as many edible bases as edible acids because most bases taste bitter. If you want to see what we mean, mix a teaspoon of baking soda in a glass of water and take just a sip. (It won't taste very good but it won't hurt you.)

Have you ever eaten too much and your stomach felt like it was trying to digest a car battery? That's acid indigestion. When people overeat and feel like they have acid indigestion, they might take an antacid. The antacid is a base, which fights the acid in your stomach and neutralizes it so it won't bother you anymore. The mixture of baking soda and water mentioned above is an effective (if yucky) antacid.

What about water? Is it an acid or a base? The answer is (drum roll, please): neither. It is neutral. On the pH scale, which tells how acidic or basic a liquid is, water is given a pH value of 7. Acidic solutions have a pH below 7. The stronger the acidity, the lower the pH, all the way down to 0. (Sounds odd, but you'll get used to it.) Basic solutions have a pH above 7. The stronger they are, the higher their pH, all the way up to 14. Why 1 to 14? It has to do with the negative logarithm business, but we're not going to worry about that here.

The bases are loaded at this level.

ammonia — Phew! This is one cap to leave on indoors.

toothpaste — Does anyone really put THIS much on their brush?

I vant to test your pH!

human blood

7.0 water - the Middle Man

coffee — I've bean brewed.

Such a dill!

vinegar

lemon juice — i'll add zest to your meal!

gastric juice — ...might be a little hard to swallow...

Experiment with pHood

1. Line up an adventuresome adult to supervise.

Why sure I'll help! Just let me park the Harley first...

2. Follow cabbage cooking instructions.

3. pHun time! Mix the cabbage juice with:

...and P is also for

photosynthesis

pitch

plasma

plate tectonics

potential energy

protein

protist

Here is a list of some common solutions and their pH. Can you tell, just from the pH, if they are acids or bases and whether they are relatively strong or relatively weak?

vinegar	2.9
lemon juice	2.3
toothpaste	9.9
coffee (black)	5.0
ammonia	11.9
blood	7.5
gastric juices (in your stomach)	1.0

There are special chemicals that change color to tell you whether a solution is an acid or a base. They are called *indicators*, and you can make one in your kitchen. Grate a red cabbage into a pot (but not an aluminum pot) and cover it with water. With adult supervision, bring the water to a boil, then simmer the cabbage for 15 minutes. Turn off the heat, let the whole shebang cool, and pour the cabbage-water mixture through a strainer to remove the cabbage (be careful not to let chemicals from your fingers pollute the cabbage juice solution).

Who said art and science are two different subjects? We made paint from the results of this experiment. Are they the same as ours? If not, what do you think it means? Try it and see what colors you get.

white vinegar · orange juice · shampoo (not real poo) · Soda Pop · vegetable juice · tomato juice · cream of tartar · baking soda · liquid soap · milk · club soda

Add a few drops of the cabbage juice to a small amount of white vinegar. What happens? Now you know what color your indicator will turn when it contacts a strong acid. Do the same with a baking soda solution. Now you know the color the indicator becomes when it mixes with a strong base. Cool, huh?! Try it with water. Now you know what happens in a neutral solution. Go ahead, test every solution you can think of. Here are a few you might not think of: orange juice, liquid soap, tomato juice, milk, shampoo, cream of tartar in water, the liquid from various canned vegetables, soda pop, unflavored soda water.

Does it surprise you to see how many familiar foods, medicines, and household substances are acids or bases?

pHantastic!

Q is for Quark

For a long time scientists have been asking questions like, "What are things made of?" When they found out that everything was made of atoms (see **A is for Atom**), they started asking, "What are atoms made of?" Eventually they discovered that atoms were made of protons, neutrons, and electrons. You've probably figured out the next question: "What are protons, neutrons, and electrons made of?"

So far it seems that electrons are just electrons. They don't seem to be made of anything else. But protons and neutrons seem to be made from smaller things even. The smaller somethings have a strange name. They're called *quarks* (pronounced "kwarks"). Quarks were discovered by a physicist named Murray Gell-Mann. He didn't exactly discover quarks the way a paleontologist discovers a new dinosaur or an astronomer discovers a new star. Instead, he made a lot of observations of how atoms behave when you smash them and do other nasty things to them, and he did a lot of math. Based on what he observed, Gell-Mann predicted that quarks exist.

The problem with quarks and other particles smaller than atoms (they're called *subatomic particles*) is that they don't act like ordinary matter, which sticks around being matter even if it changes its clothes and hairstyle. But subatomic particles sometimes turn into something else completely: energy. Einstein wrote a famous equation you've probably seen: $E = mc^2$. E stands for energy, m stands for mass, and c stands for the speed of light. What it all boils down to is this: Energy can change into mass and mass can change into energy. This doesn't happen very often with big things (except nuclear bombs), but subatomic particles do it all the time, which makes them really tricky to work with. Imagine trying to feed your baby sister if she kept changing into energy and back again. You'd never get finished in time to start your homework.

Anyway, there's lots of evidence to suggest that Gell-Mann was right, and now scientists believe that quarks really do exist. They are so small that no one can measure them or even guess their size. But Gell-Mann has figured out that they have different characteristics that he calls *flavors*. (We didn't make that up. He did.) Most of the time, there are two flavors of quarks, called *up* and *down*. (Sounds like flavors of escalators to us.) Protons have two up quarks and one down quark, while neutrons have two downs and one up. By smashing tiny atoms in gigantic machines bigger than football fields, physicists have created some other flavors of quarks, including *top* and *bottom*. Here

Convert mass into energy— today, have cereal; tomorrow, maybe...

an atomelette?

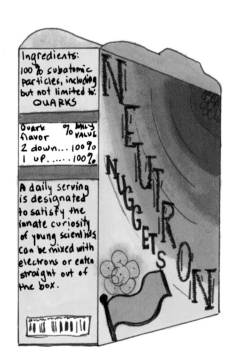

41

are our favorite quark flavors: *charm* and *strange*. We like charm quarks with chocolate sauce and whipped cream, but we prefer our strange quarks with nuts.

We know what you're thinking: What about quarks? Are they made of anything smaller? Many physicists have been wondering that, too. So far, they're not sure. They're still looking. In the meantime, they've found some other really weird subatomic particles. Like *gluons*. As their name suggests, gluons seem to be what hold quarks together. And *positrons*. Positrons are found in outer space. They're like electrons, but they have a positive charge instead of a negative charge. They're called antimatter because when a positron bumps into an electron, they destroy each other and become energy in the form of a gamma ray (which is sort of like an X ray but with an even shorter wavelength).

Remember when we said atoms are the building blocks of matter? Since atoms are made of quarks and electrons, many physicists now believe quarks and electrons are the basic building blocks of matter. But others aren't so sure. It boils down to the age-old question: If you could keep cutting a cookie into smaller bits, would you eventually come to a particle that's absolutely as small as it gets? Or do theparticles keep getting smaller and smaller and smaller and smaller...forever? Maybe you'll be the one to find out. If you do, please let us know so we can revise this book. We'll send you a free copy. And of course we'll expect you to share your Nobel Prize with us.

...and Q is also for

quadruped

quantum

quasar

R is for Rot

ANCIENT TIMES

Young King Tut is excused from the table without cleaning his plate.

– Can I go, Mummy? Ankh you very much!

After they're swept outside, the royal leftovers are broken down into atoms by bacteria and mold, then recycled into air, land, and water, over and over again.

munch munch

yum!

burp

(reeeeal close up)

Rot stinks. But without rot, life on Earth would really stink. Rot rules!

To scientists, *rot* is known as *decomposition*. Without decomposition, everything that died would stay right where it fell. Earth would be covered with huge piles of dead trees, lions, tigers, bears, dinosaurs, people, and everything else. The piles would be kilometers high. Where would anything grow? Where would anyone walk? Imagine what you'd have to wade through to go swimming at the beach. Yecch!

But aside from the unpleasantness of walking around on top of all that dead stuff, could you even exist in the first place? To answer that, think about what you are made of. Atoms. There is no "atom factory" churning out the new atoms needed to make people and cats and houses and chili corn dogs and computer games. For atoms to get inside these things, they must be recycled.

The atoms you are made of—and the atoms you breathe and drink and eat—were somewhere else before they were in you. Some were in the ground. Some were in the sky. Some were in the ocean. Some were in the carrots growing in a farmer's field. Some were in the rabbit eating the carrots. Some were in—this may sound creepy but it's true—other people. Maybe King Tut or Amelia Earhart or Elvis Presley. Or all of them (though not at the same time).

So atoms get recycled, but how? There are several ways, but one of the most important is ROT!

If your housekeeping habits are anything like ours, you can probably find a few examples of rot in your refrigerator. By keeping food cold, refrigerators delay rotting because the organisms that cause rot (the *decomposers*) work a lot slower in cold temperatures. But even in the fridge, the decomposers eventually get going. They seem to come out of nowhere, but actually they were already there, often in the form of tiny floating seed-like things called spores that landed on your food before it went into your fridge. To start growing, all they need is some food, some moisture, and a little time. Fuzzy spots of mold pop up on bread and lemons and cheese. Tiny single-celled bacteria multiply like mad, and when they get numerous enough, they give off bad-tasting, foul-smelling chemicals that ruin milk and orange juice and chicken-noodle soup.

Food isn't the only thing that rots. Just about everything that ever was alive—or is made from things that were once alive, like cotton or

Far away, and many years into the future, a few of those same atoms make their way into a banana growing on a tree. The banana is picked, shipped, sold, and made into a fried peanut butter and banana sandwich.

RECENT TIMES

– Ah thank you verra much!

The King of Rock 'n' Roll scarfs that sandwich. There are no leftovers, but as we know, that food went somewhere. As did Elvis...

There have been many kings, but only one ruler: ROT.

We're the circle...

paper (made of wood fibers)—will start to rot as soon as decomposing organisms get started. These decomposers need moisture and warm enough temperatures for their growth, which is why drying and freezing can preserve many types of food.

A mighty menagerie of organisms is ready and willing to help things rot. Think of a tree dying in the forest. This is a banquet for dozens of different decomposers, from invisible microbes to wood-eating insects to large birds that excavate nest holes. Even before the dead tree hits the ground, they begin their feast. After it falls over, the wood continues to soften and crumble. Eventually, it falls apart into tiny rotten bits that earthworms eat and poop out and churn up with other scraps of plant and animal and mineral matter.

One day, long after the tree has disappeared, you come to the spot where the rotting log had lain for years. You notice nothing. The log is part of the soil. But it is not gone. Some of its atoms have washed away to other areas. But many of them are in the soil, and they in turn will be taken up by another tree. Insects feeding on sap from the young tree may be eaten by a bird whose egg is eaten by a snake that becomes food for a fox that leaves droppings that fertilize a field of grass grazed upon by cows whose milk nourishes YOU! A part of you now contains atoms from the tree. So go the atoms of life. And death.

So, the next time you see something rotting, don't say, "Yuck!" Say, "Rot rules!"

Maybe I can't sing, but I'm still a fun guy!

...and R is also for

radio wave

radioactivity

reflection

reproduction

respiration

revolution

rotate

the circle of ROTTTT!

44

S is for Système International

Ooo-lah-lah! It sounds French. That's because it *is* French, and it's pronounced sis-TEM in-ter-NAH-see-on-AL. Even though the words are French, they refer to something used all over the world. Système International is the International System of measurement, also known as the *metric system*. If you want to sound like you know what you're talking about, call it "SI." The only trouble is that nobody in the United States (except scientists) will know what you're talking about because the United States still uses a confusing system of measurements called *customary units*. Things like inches, feet, yards, miles, cups, gallons, ounces, pounds, and degrees Fahrenheit are so-called customary units. But that is actually a very bad name, because they are customary only in the U.S.! (Okay—and two other small countries.) The rest of the world uses SI.

In SI, the basic unit of length is the meter (spelled "metre" in some countries). Find a meter stick to see how long it is. You are probably taller than a meter but not as tall as two. All other units of length are named according to how many meters (or fractions of a meter) they are equal to. A centimeter is $1/100$ of a meter. A kilometer is 1,000 meters. One of the handiest things about the metric system is that you only have to learn a few basic units (like meter, liter, gram, and degree Celsius), plus a few prefixes, to understand all the units.

"FEED THE DRAGONS," they said. HAH!

Dragon tonic takes 3/4 c. of gobbledy gook for each dragon and there were 90 of them! 3/4 cup is... 3/4 X 8 ounces equals 6 ounces; 90 dragons X 6 ounces equals 540 ounces. Since there are 128 ounces in a gallon, divide 540 by 128...so, about 4 gallons, right? **NOT!**

as in NOT ENOUGH for HUNGRY DRAGONS! As in I WAS TOAST!

Isn't there an easier way?

You mean to mix and match these units I just have to multiply or divide by 10, 100, 1,000, etc? **Easy!**

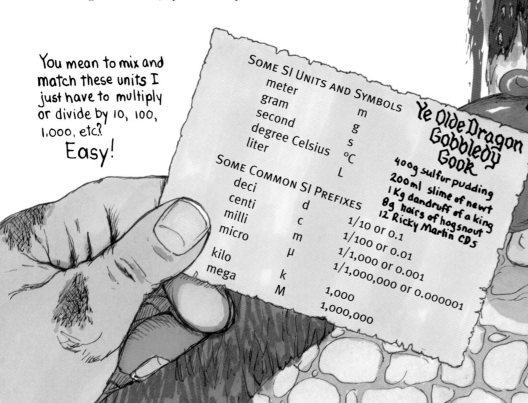

SOME SI UNITS AND SYMBOLS	
meter	m
gram	g
second	s
degree Celsius	°C
liter	L

SOME COMMON SI PREFIXES		
deci	d	1/10 or 0.1
centi	c	1/100 or 0.01
milli	m	1/1,000 or 0.001
micro	µ	1/1,000,000 or 0.000001
kilo	k	1,000
mega	M	1,000,000

Ye Olde Dragon Gobbledy Gook

400g sulfur pudding
200 ml slime of newt
1 Kg dandruff of a king
8 g hairs of hogsnout
12 Ricky Martin CDs

Ye Olde Gallon

FLUFFY

Ye Olde Happy Drag Inn

Ahhh...
200ml gobbledy gook for each of
90 dragons - that's 90 x 200ml = 18,000 ml
or 18 liters. Nothing to it!
And nothing like a good tonic,
eh Fluff?
Say, heat up my tea a bit, would
you? About 80°C would suit me fine.

...and S is also for

solid

spectrum

subatomic particle

supernova

The basic unit of mass is the gram. A large thumbtack has a mass of about one gram. A kilogram is 1,000 grams. You weigh more than 10 kilograms and less than 100 kilograms. A milligram is $^1/_{1000}$ of a gram. Even though the U.S. doesn't yet use SI units for most products, you'll find vitamins and medicines and some other things weighed in milligrams. Just look in a medicine cabinet.

The basic unit of volume, or capacity, is the liter. A liter of liquid is probably small enough for you to lift but too large for you to drink alone in one sitting—unless you're really thirsty! A deciliter is $^1/_{10}$ of a liter and a milliliter is $^1/_{1000}$ of a liter. Many small containers of liquid are measured in deciliters or milliliters, even in the U.S. See if you can find some at home or in a grocery store.

In SI, temperature is given in degrees Celsius (°C). At sea level, water freezes at 0°C and boils at 100°C. In the customary system, where temperature is measured in degrees Fahrenheit (°F), water freezes at 32°F and boils at 212°F. Logical, isn't it? No, it's not logical at all, but if you are accustomed to degrees Fahrenheit, it may seem difficult to get used to degrees Celsius. Actually, it won't take long once you start using it. Here's a little ditty that may help you understand outdoor temperatures in °C.

> Thirty is hot.
> Twenty is nice.
> Ten is chilly.
> Zero is ice.

SI is used worldwide and that alone would be a good reason to use it. But the real beauty of SI is that it makes life easier. Way easier! That's because SI is based on the *decimal system*. This makes multiplying and dividing measurements a snap.

There's one other thing about SI so cool that we must tell you. You will hardly believe it.

In the metric system, there is a connection between the units of length, mass, and volume. That may seem impossible but it's not. If you carefully measured one milliliter of water and poured it into a cube that was exactly 1 cm long x 1 cm wide x 1 cm high (or one cubic centimeter, abbreviated 1 cc), it would fill that cube exactly. That's no coincidence. But there's more. That milliliter of water has a mass of exactly one gram. (It's exact only at one temperature, 4 °C. Otherwise it weighs approximately one gram.) That's no coincidence either. It's the way the system was set up, and it makes the work of scientists easier.

If you've never used SI units before, we have some advice. Don't try to memorize what the units mean or what the prefixes mean. Just use them! Start measuring SI, talking SI, and thinking SI, and soon you'll be measuring, talking, and thinking like a scientist.

T is for Think

You've decided to enter the Big Frog Jump, so you set up a frog pen where you will raise champion jumping frogs. But one of them, Frogelina, escapes. Fortunately, Frogelina wasn't your best hopper. She couldn't even clear one meter, while some of the others hopped almost twice that far.

Six weeks later, your neighbor Francine shows you a frog that arrived in her backyard on the very day you lost Frogelina. Francine, who didn't realize you raised frogs, has been taking care of Frogelina herself. She returns the frog. You observe her and you are astonished to see that Frogelina now jumps a full two meters.

Why can Frogelina hop so much farther than before? To answer this question, you'll have to think. Thinking is the most important thing scientists do, and they have a special way of doing it. They use a series of steps called the *scientific method*. You don't need a college degree to be a scientist, and you don't need to be an adult. You just need to think like a scientist.

Asking a question is the first step of the scientific method. Your question is, "Why can Frogelina now hop so much farther than before?"

Because it's Leap Year?

The second step is to gather information that will help you answer the question. Like a detective, you search for clues. Your first thought is that Francine must have raised Frogelina differently than you did. But how? She tells you she fed Frogelina one scoop of Hop-to-It Frog Chow each day. You had been feeding her a different brand, Froggie-Bits. You suddenly have a hunch about what happened. Hop-to-It Frog Chow must improve hopping distance in frogs. A hunch like this is what scientists call a *hypothesis*. (Or in this case, a "hop-othesis".) Forming a hypothesis is the third step of the scientific method.

The next step is to test the hypothesis by performing experiments. You divide your frogs into two equal groups. One group will continue to eat FroggieBits, just like before. This is called the *control group*. The other group will eat Hop-to-It Frog Chow. This is the *experimental group*. After four weeks you will compare the average jumping ability of the two groups.

You realize that you must be careful in deciding which frogs go into which group. At the start of the experiment, you take measurements of each frog's hopping ability. You wouldn't want the best hoppers to be in one group and the worst hoppers in the other. You want to start

Welcome to the Scientific Method!

1. Ask a question: Why can Frogelina hop so much further now?

2. Gather info.

Snarf! Snarf! Hmmm...

3. Form a HOP-othesis.

Aha! It's the chow!

4. Experiment—use a control and an experimental group.

Feed Hop-to-It   Feed Froggie Bits

Rats!

Keep asking! Keep thinking! Head back to the drawing board!

5. Results do NOT support the hop-othesis.

Hooray!

5. Results support hop-othesis.

Now what? We're so glad you asked. see → p. 49

the experiment with the two groups equally matched. At the end of the experiment, you will see if the two groups still hop equally well.

You might wonder why you need to bother with a control group. Why not just feed all the frogs the new food and see if they start hopping better? If they did, the food would have to be the reason, right? Well, maybe not. Their hopping could have improved for another reason. Perhaps the weather got warmer, allowing all the frogs to leap farther. Your control group lets you observe the effect of diet alone on the frogs' jumping ability.

So, four weeks later, you remeasure all the hops. You want to see if the experimental group, eating the new food, can now out-hop the control group, still on the old food. So what do you find? We don't know. We made the whole thing up. But let's explore two possible outcomes of the frog experiment.

First imagine that after four weeks you find no difference between the two groups. On average, frogs in both groups hop the same distance. Your experiment does not support your hypothesis—in other words, your hypothesis seems to be wrong. But why did Frogelina hop farther? Maybe she found an abundance of flies to eat at Francine's house. The flies, not the chow, helped her hopping. If that's what you think, you now have a new hypothesis to test. But maybe your original hypothesis was a good one all along. Perhaps you just didn't let the experiment run long enough. It could take six weeks of eating Hop-to-It Frog Chow for hopping ability to improve. Your experiment lasted only four weeks. If this is the case, you'll have to run another experiment, designed a little differently. Here's yet another possibility: Maybe the frog that Francine found in her backyard wasn't Frogelina at all. It could have been a look-alike that arrived the same day real Frogelina disappeared. Scientists try to consider all possibilities. After testing one hypothesis, they often scrap it to try another.

Now let's suppose that after four weeks the control group is hopping about the same distance as before, and the experimental group is hopping much farther. You are thrilled! Your experiment has supported your hypothesis. So, you do what all scientists do: You tell everyone about your great discovery. The final step of the scientific method is making your results known to other people. You write an article for *Frog Hopper's Digest* in which you say that Hop-to-It Frog Chow seems to improve frog hopping ability.

But wait a minute! Your experiment has produced exciting results, and your hypothesis may be right, but are you sure that your frogs are jumping farther because of the new food? You wanted food to be the only difference between the two groups (scientists would call it the *variable* because it varies). But did you succeed? The frogs that ate Hop-to-It chow might be hoppier for a different reason. Were they getting more sunlight on their side of the pen? Did you sing, "Take Me Out to the Frog Hop" while you fed one group but not the other? Your voice could have made them hop better—or worse! Perhaps the control group wasn't perfectly controlled. Are you sure the *only* difference between them and the experimental group was the food? Believe it or not, scientists try to look for things that may be wrong with their own experiments. To be sure of what really happened, you (or someone else) will have to do the experiment again. Scientists repeat their experiments, and try to improve them each time. You might also decide to use more frogs in each group. Scientists like to use large numbers of subjects in their experiments. If you had only two or three frogs in each group, someone could say that what happened to them is not typical of all frogs. (If you know two people with red hair who are fast runners, can you say that redheads make fast runners?)

So let's suppose you repeat your experiment, and you get the same results. To get other scientists to support your hypothesis, you would want to know more about what makes frogs hop better. If you could show that a certain mineral found in Hop-to-It (but not found in FroggieBits) makes frog muscles springier, your hypothesis would be much stronger. In fact, it would have turned into a *theory*—a theory of how frog nutrition affects hopping ability. A theory is an idea based on a well-tested, well-understood hypothesis (or several related hypotheses). It's always possible that other scientists could disprove your theory through further experiments of their own.

There's only one thing that's completely certain in science: Nothing is ever completely certain. But by using the scientific method and thinking scientifically, you can be a lot more certain than uncertain.

Whew! That's a lot to think about. Hop to it!

So you got yourselves a winner AND you learned something that nobody knows. Super! The last step is...
6. communicate your results.

...and T is also for

terrestrial

transpiration

transuranium element

tsunami

typhoon

U is for Universe

Let's say you're baking cookies. You'll use flour and sugar and butter and maybe some chocolate chips or other ingredients. What are the ingredients made of? Various kinds of molecules. What are the molecules made of? Various kinds of atoms. There are about 90 kinds of atoms (not counting the ones made in laboratories), but you wouldn't want to eat most of them, and only a few are going to be found in your cookies—mostly hydrogen, oxygen, and carbon. When you've mixed all your atoms together, you put the cookie dough in the oven, heat it for a while, and pull out delicious baked cookies. The heat of the oven did not create or destroy any atoms. It might have moved some of them around, changing the way they were arranged in molecules and changing the arrangement of the molecules. But your oven cannot create or destroy atoms. It takes stars to do that.

Stars are cosmic ovens that cook hydrogen atoms at temperatures in the millions of degrees Celsius. Hydrogen atoms are the simplest and lightest of all atoms, and at super high temperatures, they become so overcooked that they start to fuse to each other to become heavier atoms. Some of those heavier atoms (like oxygen and carbon) are in your cookies.

But where did the hydrogen atoms come from? They came from the *Big Bang*.

Once upon a time—actually, it was somewhere around fifteen billion years ago—there was no space and no time. This was before the beginning of time, if you can imagine that, and in a place that wasn't a place at all, since there were no places. We admit we have a hard time imagining such nothingness, but astronomers think that all of the matter, all of the energy, and even all of the empty space now filling most of the universe were once smushed together in an incredibly small space, at incredibly high temperature and pressure.

And then there was an ENORMOUS explosion. Scientists call it the Big Bang. Nobody really understands what happened, but within almost no time at all, the universe contained all the protons and neutrons and electrons that would eventually become galaxies and stars and planets and people and chocolate chip cookies.

The protons attracted the electrons and pretty soon there was atom soup. While this was happening, the universe was travelling outward in all directions. Early on, the atoms made a uniform cloud of particles, but as the universe expanded, it cooled…and as it cooled it got a little lumpy. Some parts contained more matter than others, and they combined to form gases, which had gravity that attracted more gases, making bigger lumps with more gravity that cooled further and clumped more to become galaxies. Inside the galaxies, much smaller particle clouds collapsed into themselves. The gas molecules inside these clouds collided with such force that they began to fuse in a nuclear reaction that gave off heat and light. Stars were born.

As swirling clumps of gas formed into stars, some of them spit out a few chunks of solid matter, but the stars' gravity kept those chunks from flying too far. The result was a balance that forced the chunks to revolve around their stars. Today those chunks are known as planets.

The universe has not stopped expanding since the moment of the Big Bang. Everything is getting farther and farther away from everything else. In fact, there is recent evidence that the expansion rate is speeding up. Will the universe continue to expand forever? Or will it eventually stop? And if it does, what next? Will the universe start to pull itself together, getting smaller and smaller until. . . until what? Until there is a Big Crunch—the opposite of the Big Bang? And then what? Will there be a sequel to the Big Bang? Big Bang 2?? Have there been many Big Bangs, alternating with Big Crunches in a never-ending cycle?

These questions have yet to be answered. You can contemplate them as you nibble on the chocolate chip cookies whose protons, neutrons, and electrons all had their origin in the Big Bang. You are contemplating the universe. We can think of nothing better.

Wow! These earthlings sure know how to arrange protons, neutrons, and electrons!

...and U is also for

ultraviolet (UV)

unicellular

urine

V is for Vortex

What do tornados and the water running out of your bathtub have in common? If you like scary stories, read on.

Imagine you are swimming in an enormous bathtub with thousands of other people and suddenly someone pulls the giant plug in the bottom of the pool. Because everyone was already swimming in some direction or other, they will keep travelling the way they were going even as the suction pulls them toward the drain. The result is that you and all your friends will be on a spiraling path toward the plug hole.

Okay, chances are you'll never be sucked down a giant drain, but something similar happens all the time.

As you just saw, fluids don't flow straight down the drain. They flow in a spiraling motion called a *vortex*. Air is a fluid, too, and can form a vortex. In the summertime, this happens frequently within thunderstorm clouds. If a vortex of air in a thundercloud snakes down and touches the ground, it is called a tornado, or a twister.

A large twister may have wind speeds of 200 or 300 miles per hour. The speed of the whirling wind can cause tremendous damage, and the low pressure inside the winds can pick up houses, barns, cows, cars, and people and their dogs—the most famous being Dorothy and Toto. Some people have said that a tornado can pull the feathers off a chicken. We don't believe it. . . but you never know!

Speaking of not believing things, many people think water runs down the drain counterclockwise in the Northern Hemisphere (north of the equator) and clockwise in the Southern Hemisphere (south of the equator). This has led many people to wonder what the water does if it's right on the equator. Does it go straight down? Actually, this whole notion is bogus. Because of the earth's rotation, some weather systems make a counterclockwise circle north of the equator and a clockwise circle south of the equator. But the earth's rotation has little effect on the water in your bathtub. It is the small wobbles caused by your movements in the tub that set the water spinning down the drain one way or the other. The most interesting thing about the bathtub myth is that so many people believe it. Scientific knowledge is based on evidence from observations. It is not difficult to observe that, wherever you are on Earth, water can flow down the drain in either direction. But one thing's for sure: It will always flow down in a vortex.

Hmph. Tornadoes! I bet you can guess what I'LL want from the Wizard!

...and V is also for

vapor

vertebrate

virus

W is for "Wow"!

Science is full of things that make us say, "Wow!" Here's a "wowful" fact (we made up that word but not this fact): If our galaxy, the Milky Way, were shrunk to the size of North America, our solar system (the Sun and its nine planets) would fit inside a coffee cup.

It's sort of like that with science in general. This book covers just an itsy-bitsy-teenie-weenie fraction of a fraction of all we know about science, which in turn is probably just a tiny fraction of all the scientific knowledge there is to know.

Here's another wowful fact: When a honey bee finds nectar-rich flowers, it goes back to the hive to tell the other bees where to find the food. It communicates the information by way of a special dance that tells the other bees which way to go and how far.

In a way, wowsome facts are candy for the brain—tasty for a moment, but of no lasting value. But you can make them a nutritious meal if you understand the science behind them. Here's a fact: An eye doctor can look into the eyes of a bald man and tell him what color hair he had as a child. Wow! But how can that be? The retina at the back of your eye has colored layers that reflect how much skin pigment you had at a younger age. Young children with light-colored skin also have light-colored hair. As they grow older, their hair color and skin color can change, but their inner eye color does not. So an eye doctor can peer into the eye of a bald or gray-haired man, see a light yellow retina, and amaze the patient by saying, "You were a blonde little boy, weren't you?" That's not just a wowzy fact. It's scientific understanding!

Wowmazing facts also become more nourishing when we see how they affect our lives. Take water. Just about everything else gets more dense as it freezes. But water gets less dense as it freezes. That means ice forming in water will float on top of that water. If ice sank, there would not be life as we know it on Earth! All the ice formed in lakes and oceans would sink to the bottom. Year after year, more and more ice would build up and summer heat would not be enough to melt it. The oceans would get so cold that the entire Earth would have an arctic climate. . . . Brrrrrr! And you just bought a new bathing suit. See how one wow leads to another? Wow on!

Let fun facts begin WOWnderful journeys! Take WOWter, for instance—

Uh, I get less dense when I chill out! BUT! Let's say H_2O is densest at 0° C. What would happen? Or, what wouldn't?

Ice would sink.

Have you seen my snack?

Ice fishing couldn't happen in Minnesota, and polar bears couldn't ride icebergs.

Later, the ice would be so thick, nothing would get warm. It would be winter all the time. The earth would be a Total North Pole.

The sun would melt a little ice and it would snow, but there would be no snowman because...

no cotton to weave a cap

no coal to dig for eyes

no carrots to grow for a nose

no wool to knit for a muffler

no trees to grow for stick arms

no leather to tan for a baseball or mitt

no one to roll big balls of snow. No us.

Nothing we know and love would be around.

But, lucky for us, ice floats.

Aren't you glad?

...and W is also for

warm-blooded

water

wave

wavelength

work

whew!

53

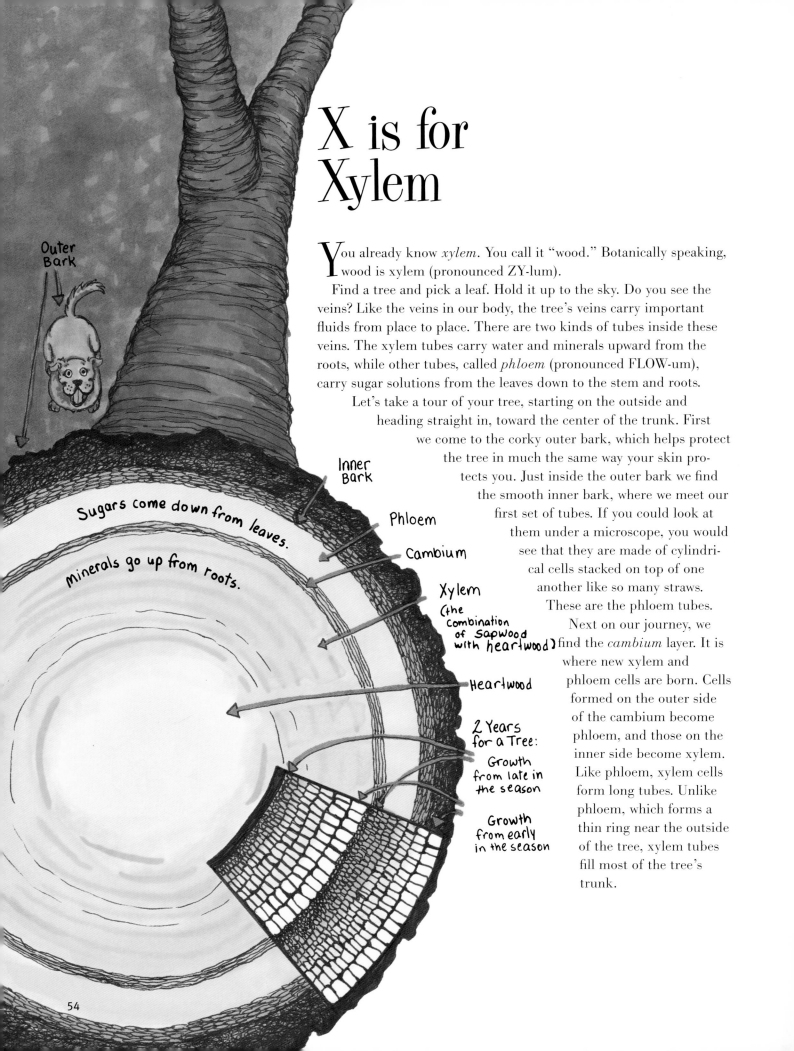

X is for Xylem

Outer Bark

You already know *xylem*. You call it "wood." Botanically speaking, wood is xylem (pronounced ZY-lum).

Find a tree and pick a leaf. Hold it up to the sky. Do you see the veins? Like the veins in our body, the tree's veins carry important fluids from place to place. There are two kinds of tubes inside these veins. The xylem tubes carry water and minerals upward from the roots, while other tubes, called *phloem* (pronounced FLOW-um), carry sugar solutions from the leaves down to the stem and roots.

Let's take a tour of your tree, starting on the outside and heading straight in, toward the center of the trunk. First we come to the corky outer bark, which helps protect the tree in much the same way your skin protects you. Just inside the outer bark we find the smooth inner bark, where we meet our first set of tubes. If you could look at them under a microscope, you would see that they are made of cylindrical cells stacked on top of one another like so many straws. These are the phloem tubes.

Next on our journey, we find the *cambium* layer. It is where new xylem and phloem cells are born. Cells formed on the outer side of the cambium become phloem, and those on the inner side become xylem. Like phloem, xylem cells form long tubes. Unlike phloem, which forms a thin ring near the outside of the tree, xylem tubes fill most of the tree's trunk.

Inner Bark

Phloem

Cambium

Xylem
(the combination of sapwood with heartwood)

Heartwood

2 Years for a Tree:

Growth from late in the season

Growth from early in the season

Sugars come down from leaves.

minerals go up from roots.

Back to the tour. Once we've left the cambium, we enter the central part of the trunk. If you put your hand on this part of a freshly cut stump, it would get wet from sap oozing out of the xylem tubes. This part of the trunk is called *sapwood*. It consists of xylem cells that conduct water and dissolved minerals upward to the tree's branches and leaves. Further in, at the very center of the trunk, we find another section of xylem tubes, which may look darker than the sapwood. This is the *heartwood*. The xylem cells in heartwood no longer conduct fluid, but they do help support the tree's enormous weight. In many big trees, most of the trunk is heartwood.

Our tour is complete, but you should know that there is a lot of variation in trees. We described a typical oak or maple, but not all trees are set up exactly this way. Plants other than trees also have xylem and phloem tubes, but they may be arranged a little differently.

Now here's a hard question: Why is wood hard? The walls of xylem cells contain substances called cellulose and lignin that make itty-bitty xylem cells tough enough to be turned into chairs and pianos and baseball bats.

Got time for one more tour? We're going to travel through one year in the life of a tree. We'll start in the spring. As the days lengthen and the temperatures start to climb, the cambium starts producing phloem and xylem cells. The xylem cells grow quickly. Their cell walls are thin and light in color. As spring turns to summer, the cambium keeps on making xylem cells, but they have thicker, darker walls. Come fall and winter, the cambium takes a break. Next spring, new thin-walled cells will appear.

This is how a tree gets rings. Each year brings a new ring of light-colored cells grading into dark-colored ones. You can tell the age of a tree by counting its rings.

Find a large tree stump. Starting on the outside, you can count one ring for every year of your life, until you come to the ring that was born the same year you were. Keep counting rings and you may find those that were laid down when your parents were born—maybe even your grandparents. If your stump is large enough, you can find wood that was made when the American Revolution began (1776), or when Columbus sailed the ocean blue (1492). Cool, don't you think? Just remember what these rings really are: xylem.

Maybe you're wondering why people call it "wood" instead of "xylem." We've wondered too, and the best we can come up with is that "xylem" just doesn't roll off the tongue. Quick, say this ten times fast: "How much xylem would a xylemchuck chuck if a xylemchuck could chuck xylem?"

Every year the cambium makes new cells and trees grow wider. But trees only grow up from their tips. That means a scar stays at the height it was made!

30-year-old Grandpappy Xylemchuck nibble

brand-spankin'new Junior Xylemchuck nibble (in progress)

...and X is also for

X ray

— What makes boys the way we are?
  —Y.
— Because I wondered.
  —No, I mean **Y.** It's the chromosome.
— That short little deal make us boys?
  —Yep.
— Why?
  —Yeah. **Y.**
— No, WHY?
  —Well, I'm not sure exactly, but it
   has something to do with your **Y.**
— And what have you got?
  —X
— And I don't have X?
  —Oh, you do, too.
— But I'm a boy and you're a girl.
  So how can I have it, too?
  —No, I have two. Two X's, that
   is. You have one X and one **Y.**
— Who says?
  —Dad says.
— I never heard him say anything
  about it.
  —Well, he didn't exactly say it.
   He did it.
— Did what?
  —Gave you your **Y.**
— But he's your dad, too. So he
  must have given you one, too,
  right?
  —Wrong. Just read this thing
   and you'll see.

Y is for
Y Chromosome

This is about sex. Your sex. It's about whether you are a boy or a girl—and why. Do you know why? The answer may surprise you: because of your father. Don't get us wrong. Your dad didn't decide whether you were to be a boy or a girl. But he is responsible just the same.

Almost every cell in the human body has 23 pairs of chromosomes, for a total of 46 (see **D is for DNA**). Way before you were born, sperm and egg cells were made in your parents' bodies. If they had each contained 46 chromosomes, when the sperm and the egg joined to make the single cell that grew to be you, you would have had twice that many chromosomes, 92. And if you ever had a child with someone else who had 92 chromosomes, that child would have 184 chromosomes. Soon the cells would be crowded and chaotic. Obviously, this system would not work.

What happens is that certain cells, called *germ cells* (not to be confused with the kinds of germs that make you sick), in the ovaries of a woman and the testes of a man divide in a special way. Like all the other cells in the body, they start with 46 chromosomes in 23 pairs, but when they're finished they have half that many chromosomes. In this special process, called *meiosis* (pronounced my-O-sis), the 23 pairs of chromosomes line up, then the two chromosomes in each pair say good-bye to each other and part company. One goes one way while the other goes the opposite way. Then the cell itself divides in half, so that there are 23 chromosomes in each new cell. These chromosomes are not in pairs. But when the 23 chromosomes of a father's sperm meet the 23 chromosomes of a mother's egg, they

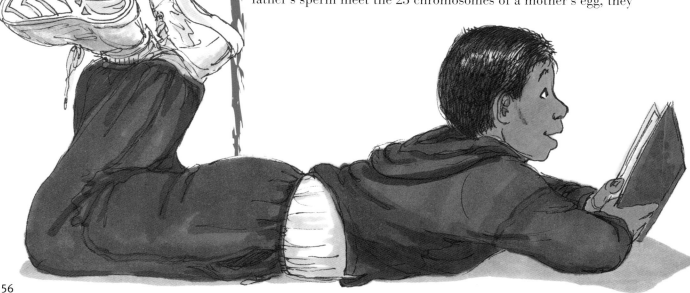

come together to create a cell with 46 chromosomes, now in 23 pairs. This cell will soon replicate to create new cells, but it will not split the number of chromosomes in half. Instead, each new cell will have 23 pairs of chromosomes. So the cells of children have the same number of chromosomes as their parents, not twice as many.

Through a microscope, the two chromosomes in each pair look pretty much the same. But there is an exception—the *sex chromosomes*. If you are male, the two sex chromosomes look completely different. One of them is normal-sized. It's called the *X chromosome*. The other is much shorter. It's called the *Y chromosome*. If you are female, the two chromosomes do look the same. Both are full-sized X chromosomes. Females have no Y chromosome. We say that males are XY (one X chromosome and one Y chromosome), while females are XX (two X chromosomes).

So what makes you male or female? Remember, in your mother both sex chromosomes are Xs. So when a mother's germ cell makes two egg cells, they each get an X chromosome. There are no other choices. But in your father there is an X chromosome and a Y chromosome. So when the father's germ cell divides to make two sperm cells, one will get an X chromosome and the other will get a Y.

Now let's skip to the moment of conception. That's when one of your father's sperm cells met one of your mother's egg cells. If the sperm had an X chromosome, the fertilized egg would have two Xs, one from each of your parents. So, you would be female. If the sperm had a Y, it would join the X in your mother's egg, and the fertilized egg would be XY. You would be male. There is an equal chance that fertilized eggs will be XY or XX, which is why the number of boy babies and girl babies is almost exactly the same. So, you are a boy or you are a girl for only one reason: because of your father. You might want to thank him some day.

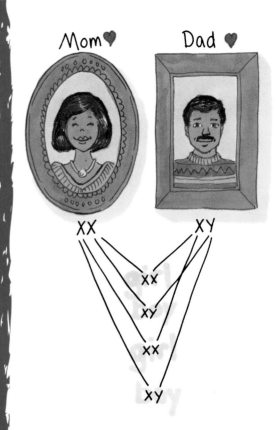

When we write, we make the Xs and Ys the same size, but they really aren't! This is a better comparison:

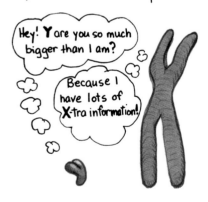

Hey! Y are you so much bigger than I am?

Because I have lots of X-tra information!

...and Y is also for

year

yes!

yolk

57

Z is for Zzzzzzzzzz

Having the time of your life? Maybe so!

going anywhere: travel

Watching TV you claim is "educational"

Chores

School

watching TV that really is educational!

on the phone

going to the movies

daydreaming

babysitting

snacking

reading good books, like this one!

on the computer

hanging out at the mall

hassling your big sister

homework (it just FEELS like more)

Ahhh, SLEEP!

exercize, like soccer or blading or dancing or just walking around

Hotbeds of Electrical Activity

-You're saying there's activity in my SISTER'S brain? NO WAY!

We're not trying to put you to sleep, but we thought we would end this book by talking about sleep. It's an activity that occupies about one-third of most people's lives. That means that if you live to 80, you'll spend a total of about 250,000 hours, or 10,000 days, or 27 years, sleeping! That's more than the amount of time you would spend walking, eating, reading, or (we hope) watching TV. So sleep must be pretty important. But what is it?

There are scientists who spend a good deal of time trying to answer that question and other questions about sleep. They want to know things like, how do people fall asleep and how do they wake up? Is sleep necessary? What happens in your brain and other parts of your body during sleep? What can people do to sleep better if they have a sleep disorder like insomnia (the inability to sleep)? Does your bubblegum get stale on the bedpost overnight?

Answers to most of these questions have come about through research in sleep laboratories, where volunteers allow researchers to tape sensitive electrodes to their heads before they bed down. The electrodes are attached to wires that run to a machine called an *electroencephalo-graph*, or EEG for short. Does this sound like a fun way to go to sleep, or would you rather just curl up with a good book in your own bed?

Believe it or not, your brain is a hotbed of electrical activity. There are about a trillion nerve cells, or *neurons*, in there. Neurons send and receive information that's needed to stay alive (like the signals that control your heart and lungs), and they are also used for more advanced luxuries like complex thoughts. An electric signal moving through a nerve is kind of like water moving through a hose—but not exactly. Instead of water, the signal is an electrical charge. The signal can be picked up by an EEG and recorded on paper as squiggly lines that actually look a little like waves. These patterns are called brain waves.

Your brain waves have certain patterns when you are awake that change when you fall asleep. Thanks to sleep volunteers, we have learned that there are five different stages of sleep. The first four stages have very creative names: Stage One, Stage Two, Stage Three, and Stage Four. (Are you asleep yet?) As you drift off, you enter Stage One, a very light sleep. If you were awakened during Stage One sleep, you would not even realize you were sleeping. But you are more relaxed and your heart rate is slower than it is when you're awake. On an EEG, your brain waves appear smaller and slower.

In Stage Two, your brain waves slow down further, but still have sudden bursts of activity. About 45 minutes after falling asleep, you enter a deeper state of sleep, Stage Three. Stage Four is the deepest yet, with very long brain waves and very little body movement. But after just a few minutes in Stage Four, you start working backwards to Stage Three, then Stage Two, then. . . no, not Stage One, but

Possible Sleep Volunteer
(still awake—but just had lunch)

alert brain waves →   ← sleep brain waves

something else entirely. In this new stage of sleep, you begin to dream.

Whether or not you remember dreaming, you do it every night, and while you are dreaming, something interesting happens to your eyes. They dart around beneath your eyelids, as if you were awake and "looking" at your dreams. The dream stage of sleep is called the *Rapid Eye Movement* stage, or *REM* sleep. During REM sleep, your breathing is irregular and your heart rate increases. Brain waves look pinched—more like the brain waves from a person who is awake. Ironically, even though your brain may seem more active, the rest of your body is very relaxed. After dreaming for 20 minutes or more, you drift back into Stage Two, then Three, then Four, etc. The sleep cycle repeats four to six times a night, but as the night goes along, the dreaming periods get longer while the deep, non-dreaming sleep stages become shorter. Then the alarm clock goes off and it's time to get ready for school. Too bad! You were dreaming they banned homework.

Did you ever dream that falling asleep could be so complicated?

Stage One Sleep
(unaware of state)

brain waves start to change

Stage Two Sleep
(clearly relaxed)

brain waves slower with sudden active bursts

Stage Three Sleep
(almost there...)

waves spread apart

Stage Four Sleep (out like a light)

slow, jagged waves; still body

REM Sleep

the body is still, but the brain is rockin'

Hey! We said REM, not RAM!

...and Z is also for

zenith

zero gravity

zygote

Glossary

ABSOLUTE ZERO The temperature at which molecules stop moving—approximately –273.16 degrees C. Nothing has ever been quite this cold. But in the lab, scientists have reached temperatures within a few millionths of a degree of absolute zero. That's cold enough for us! Absolutely!

AIR PRESSURE (also called **ATMOSPHERIC PRESSURE**) The pressure that air molecules create by bombarding everything they come in contact with. Air pressure pushes up, down, and sideways. Rubber suction cups work because there is little air under the cup and lots of air on top of it, and that air pressure holds the cup in place. Air pressure is highest at sea level and gets lower as you go up in altitude.

AMOEBA A microscopic single-celled organism with a jellylike body. Amoebas move by extending their pseudopods, or "false feet," which are actually part of their bodies and have no fixed shape. Amoebas can cause a serious digestive disease in humans called dysentery.

ATMOSPHERE The mixture of gases surrounding the earth or another planet. By far the most abundant gas in the earth's atmosphere is nitrogen (78%). Oxygen is second (21%). The remaining 1% includes argon, carbon dioxide, and traces of many other gases.

ATOMIC WEIGHT The number that represents the mass of an atom. Carbon is given an atomic weight of exactly 12 and all other atoms are compared with carbon. Hydrogen, the lightest element, has an atomic weight of 1, and Lawrencium, with an atomic weight of 103, is the heaviest element known. So far.

AXON The long, thin part of a nerve cell, or neuron. (See Nerve Cell.) Axons carry electrical impulses away from the cell body. Most axons are measured in millimeters, but there are some running from the base of the spine to the tip of the toes that can be a meter long in some people! If you thought all cells were tiny, think again!

BACTERIUM (plural **BACTERIA**) One-celled organisms with no distinct nucleus. Bacteria reproduce by dividing in half. Some bacteria cause deadly diseases in humans, yet others are helpful. Bacteria can be shaped like spheres, rods, spirals, or commas. (So far, no bacteria shaped like question marks have been discovered!)

BAROMETER An instrument used to measure air pressure, a factor useful in predicting changes in the weather. When the barometer reading drops (meaning air pressure is going down), a storm may be approaching.

BIOME The community of plants and animals typically found in a certain climatic region. Grasslands, deserts, tropical rain forests, and tundras are four very distinct biomes with four very distinct sets of inhabitants.

BOHR MODEL A description of the hydrogen atom by Danish physicist Niels Bohr which said the electron in a hydrogen atom is restricted to circular orbits around the nucleus, as opposed to the now accepted "cloud" pattern.

BOIL To change from a liquid state to a gaseous state by heating. The boiling point of a liquid is the hottest it can get (unless you increase the air pressure, which is what a pressure cooker does). The opposite of boiling is condensing. (See Condense.)

CELL The microscopic building block of life. The human body has more than 100 trillion cells. Structures called organelles inside the cell carry out the cell's functions. Simple cells lack a nucleus, or "control center," while more advanced cells have them.

CHEMICAL BOND The way atoms join together to make molecules. In covalent bonds, the atoms share electrons. In ionic bonds, one atom gives up one or more electrons and another atom accepts those electrons. The first atom becomes positively charged and the other one becomes negatively charged.

CHEMICAL REACTION The change in the arrangement of atoms and molecules that occurs when two or more substances react. The resulting substances can be very different from those that reacted. Nitrogen and hydrogen react to form ammonia, a substance with properties completely unlike nitrogen or hydrogen.

COLD-BLOODED Refers to an animal whose body temperature reflects the temperature of its surroundings and changes as the outside temperature changes. Cold-blooded animals have some ways of regulating their temperature, but they cannot generate heat from within their bodies. Fish, amphibians, and reptiles are all cold-blooded. "Poikilothermic" and "ectothermic" are synonyms for cold-blooded. See also Warm-Blooded.

COMPOUND Two or more elements that are combined into a molecule that has properties different from those of its components. Water is a compound made of the elements hydrogen and oxygen. Salt is a compound made of sodium and chlorine.

CONDENSE To change from a gaseous state to a liquid state by cooling. The opposite of condensation is boiling. (See Boil.)

COVALENT BOND See Chemical Bond.

DECIBEL A unit that measures sound or noise levels (abbreviated dB). A sound that you can hardly hear has 0 dB, while a jet plane taking off has 110–140 dB. Sounds of more than 140 dB can damage your hearing.

DENSITY A comparison between a substance's mass and its volume. If a certain volume of substance A has more mass than the same volume of substance B, we say substance A has a higher density than substance B. A bag of sand is more massive than the same size bag of cotton, so sand is denser than cotton.

DIFFRACTION The bending of a light ray as it passes by the edge of something in its path or through a pinhole.

EGG The reproductive cell of female animals. To develop, an egg must be fertilized by a sperm cell. Also, a fertilized egg, such as those laid by fish, amphibians, or reptiles. Eggs of birds and reptiles have hard shells that maintain a moist environment inside.

ELECTROMAGNETIC RADIATION (or **ELECTROMAGNETIC WAVES**) Energy that travels through space in the form of waves. Electromagnetic waves have magnetic and electric energy, and in some ways behave like waves and in other ways like particles. Light, radio waves, microwaves, television signals, heat waves, X-rays, and cosmic rays are all forms of electromagnetic radiation.

ENERGY The ability to do work. There are several kinds of energy, including heat, light, chemical energy, mechanical energy, and nuclear energy. Energy cannot be created or destroyed, but it can be changed from one form to another.

ENZYME A complex molecule that aids in many chemical reactions within the cell. Although enzymes control chemical reactions, they are not changed by them. There are about 3,000 different enzymes in the average human cell.

FERTILIZATION In animal or plant reproduction, the act of combining a male reproductive cell and a female reproductive cell. When the male reproductive cell fertilizes the female cell, a zygote results, which develops into a new organism.

FLUID A substance that flows and takes the shape of its container. Gases and liquids are fluids.

FLUORESCENCE The ability some substances have to give off light when they are exposed to certain electromagnetic waves.

FORCE The push or pull that causes an object to move or change its motion. One important force, gravity, operates at a distance. The gravitational force of the Moon on Earth causes the tides. Other forces called "contact forces" occur when two objects touch each other.

When bat hits ball, a contact force operates on both. Forces are measured in newtons. (See S is for Système International.)

FREEZE To change from a liquid state to a solid state by cooling. When water freezes, it becomes ice. The opposite of freezing is melting. (See Melt.)

FREQUENCY The number of cycles per second in a wave, that is, how many waves pass a certain point in one second. Frequency is measured in Hertz (Hz)—one cycle per second is equal to 1 Hz. In sound waves, pitch (how "high" or "low" a note is) is determined by wave frequency. In light waves, color is determined by frequency.

FUNGUS (plural **FUNGI**) A kind of organism that in some ways seems like a plant, but has no leaves, no flowers, and no chlorophyll. Unlike plants, fungi cannot make their own food, so they feed off dead or decaying plants and animals. Mushrooms, molds, yeast, and mildews are all types of fungi.

FUSION In physics, the joining of atom nuclei to make a heavier nucleus. In the process of fusion, huge amounts of energy are released. In chemistry, fusion is the melting of a solid into a liquid. The process is often used to make a new substance by melting other substances together.

GAMETE A reproductive cell, like an egg or a sperm.

GAMMA RAY An electromagnetic ray with a very high frequency and a very short wavelength. Gamma rays can penetrate thick iron or concrete. They are harmful to people, but they can be used by doctors to kill cancer cells.

GAS One of the three common states of matter (the others being liquid and solid). A gas expands to fill the volume and shape of its container (like the clutter in some people's rooms). The molecules of a gas are moving rapidly. Air is a mixture of gases, mostly nitrogen. When the temperature of a gas is lowered enough, it becomes a liquid.

GENE A section of DNA carrying information about one or more traits. Genes are passed from parent to offspring.

G-FORCE A way of measuring the force felt from gravity. At rest on Earth's surface, the force of gravity is said to be 1 g. The actual force will be the body's weight. When an astronaut lifts off, she feels a force of several g's—meaning several times her resting weight on Earth. In orbit, she feels a force of 0 g because she is falling freely.

HABITAT The environment in which a community of organisms normally lives. For example, the marine habitat is home to many living things. The rocky seashore is a different habitat with different plants and animals.

HEAT A form of energy associated with the movement of molecules. The faster molecules move, the more heat they generate. Heat can be passed from one object to another. It can also be changed into other forms of energy.

HYDROCARBON A chemical that contains only hydrogen and carbon. Most common fuels, like petroleum and natural gas, are hydrocarbons.

INERTIA An object's tendency to resist changes in motion. If it is still, it wants to remain still. If it is in motion, it wants to continue moving at the same speed and in the same direction. In order for an object to change its speed or direction of motion, it must be acted upon by a force. Friction is often the force that slows moving things.

INFRARED Electromagnetic rays that have wavelengths a little bit longer than those of red light. These waves are invisible to the human eye, but can be felt as heat. Most of the heat from the Sun and from lightbulbs is infrared radiation.

INORGANIC See Organic.

INVERTEBRATE An animal with no backbone (as opposed to a vertebrate). There are many groups of invertebrates, among them mollusks (including clams and snails), arthropods (including insects

and crustaceans), echinoderms (including sea stars) and annelids (including earthworms).

IONIC BOND See Chemical Bond.

ISOTOPE There are varying numbers of neutrons within the atoms of most elements. These atoms are called isotopes of those elements. For example, isotopes of zinc can have anywhere from 34 to 40 neutrons. Since the number of neutrons affects an atom's stability, some isotopes break down or decay and give off radioactive energy. These isotopes can be dangerous but they can also be used to treat diseases and date fossils.

JET STREAM The high-altitude air current that usually moves from west to east around the earth at speeds of 150–500 kilometers per hour. The jet stream affects weather patterns around the world.

JOINT A place in the body where two or more bones are connected to each other and move freely. In plants, a joint is where a branch or leaf grows out of the stem.

KELVIN A unit in the Kelvin temperature scale. One degree Kelvin is the same as one degree Celsius, but in the Kelvin scale, zero degrees (known as "absolute zero") is the temperature at which molecules stop moving. This is the coldest temperature possible (–273.15 degrees C, or –459.67 degrees F), but nothing has ever been made quite that cold (except for David's bedroom when he lived in Edinburgh, Scotland).

KERATIN A hard protein found mainly in the body's outer layers. Skin, hair, and nails are all made of keratin.

KINETIC ENERGY The energy of moving objects, whether they be as tiny as molecules or as large as ocean waves.

KINGDOM In the classification of living things, kingdoms are the highest level of division. Years ago, organisms were placed in one of two kingdoms: plant or animal. Today, most scientists use a classification scheme that has five kingdoms: plants, animals, fungi, protists, and monerans.

LASER (Light Amplification by Stimulated Emission of Radiation) A device that produces an extremely intense and narrowly focused beam of light. Lasers are used to perform eye surgery, calculate the distance between Earth and the Moon, operate CD players, and much more.

LAW In science, a law is a statement of something that always happens. Newton's Third Law of Motion states that for every action there is an equal and opposite reaction. Boyle's Law explains how gases behave at certain temperatures and pressures.

LIPID A type of compound that does not dissolve in water. Lipids include fats, oils, and waxes. They are found in all animals and plants.

LIQUID One of the three common states of matter (along with gas and solid). A liquid does not have a definite shape but it has a definite volume.

LUMINESCENCE Light given off without much heat. Bioluminescence is a cool light given off by living creatures. Many bioluminescent creatures are single-celled, but others, such as fireflies and certain fungi, are more complex.

LUNAR Relating to the Moon. A lunar month is the time it takes the Moon to revolve one time around the earth. A lunar eclipse occurs when the earth casts a shadow on the Moon.

MAMMAL A class of warm-blooded vertebrates whose females give birth to live young and nurse them with milk produced in mammary glands. Most mammals have hair or fur. Mice, cows, whales, monkeys, dogs, bats, and humans are all mammals. Some people say "animal" when they mean "mammal," but many kinds of animals are not mammals. (All mammals are animals, however.) See also Vertebrate.

MEIOSIS The kind of cell division that produces two reproductive cells from one parent cell. Each reproductive cell has half the number of chromosomes of the parent cell. The reproductive cells will be sperm cells if produced in a male animal and egg cells, or "ova," if produced in a female animal; in plants they will be pollen (male) or ovules (female). Compare with Mitosis.

MELT To change from a solid state to liquid state by heating. Ice melts to form water. The opposite of melting is freezing. (See Freeze.)

MINERAL Usually refers to an inorganic substance that has a definite chemical composition and a crystal form. Sometimes the term "mineral" refers to any natural material that can be mined, including coal and petroleum, which are organic materials.

MITOSIS The kind of cell division in which one parent cell produces two identical daughter cells, with the same number of chromosomes. This is the normal way cells divide as an organism grows. Compare with Meiosis.

MOLECULE Two or more atoms attached to each other by chemical bonding. A molecule of hydrochloric acid (HCl) has one atom of hydrogen and one atom of chlorine. A molecule of water (H_2O) has two atoms of hydrogen and one atom of oxygen. Sometimes atoms of the same element bond to each other. These are molecules, too. One molecule of oxygen gas (O_2) has two atoms of oxygen linked to each other.

MOMENTUM A measure of an object's motion. Momentum is equal to the object's mass multiplied by its velocity. A small object moving quickly might have the same momentum as a massive object moving slowly.

MOON A heavenly body that orbits a planet. The earth has one moon, simply called the Moon. Some other planets have numerous moons. Jupiter has at least 16 and Saturn has at least 21.

NATURAL HISTORY The study of living things (and nonliving things found in nature, like rocks and clouds), especially their evolutionary relationships.

NERVE CELL An elongated cell that conducts electric impulses between the brain or spinal cord and other parts of the body.

NEURON A nerve cell.

NUCLEUS In physics and chemistry, the nucleus is the positively charged center of an atom, containing almost all the atom's mass. In biology, it is the flattened sphere in cells that contains the cell's genetic material.

ORBIT The path of a celestial body around another. For example, the earth and the other planets of our solar system orbit the Sun. Many planets, including Earth, are orbited by one or more moons.

ORGANELLES Tiny structures within cells that perform functions essential to life. If you think of a cell as a "factory," the organelles are its machines. The nucleus is an organelle, and so are ribosomes (where proteins are made), mitochondria (where food substances are broken down to provide energy), vacuoles (where materials are stored), and, in plants, chloroplasts (where photosynthesis takes place).

ORGANIC In chemistry, organic refers to a compound that contains carbon. In biology, it refers to anything that is or was once living, or anything produced by a living thing. Wood is organic, whether the tree it comes from is living or dead. Metal is not organic. It is not and never was living, and it was not produced by a living thing. (Things that are not organic are referred to as inorganic.)

OSMOSIS The movement of molecules through a membrane in order to make the concentration of molecules equal on both sides of the membrane. This is the main way that nutrients and wastes pass in and out of cells.

OVARY In animals, the female organ that produces egg cells. In plants, the female organ that produces ovules, which develop into seeds.

OVUM (plural **OVA**) An egg cell, or female gamete. When fertilized by a male gamete, it becomes a zygote.

OZONE A molecule containing three atoms of oxygen (O_3), rather than the more common form of only two atoms (O_2). Unlike O_2, ozone has a strong odor, which you may be able to smell after a lightning storm as ozone is produced when electricity moves through air. There is a natural layer of ozone in the upper atmosphere that absorbs ultraviolet radiation from the Sun. These rays can be damaging to people and other organisms.

PHOTOSYNTHESIS The process used by plants to make their own food. The essential ingredients are water and carbon dioxide and the energy of sunlight. Chlorophyll is also needed for photosynthesis, and green plants have it. Animals breathe the oxygen produced by plants and they eat plants (or they eat other animals that eat plants), so animals also depend on photosynthesis.

PITCH The property of sound that depends on its frequency, or number of vibrations per second. We speak of pitch as being "higher" or "lower." The higher the frequency, the higher the pitch. If a string is made thinner or shorter, it will vibrate with a higher pitch.

PLASMA In biology, the clear part of the blood consisting mostly of water, in which the blood cells move. In physics, plasma is a fourth state of matter (other than solid, liquid, or gas) made of electrically charged particles and found within stars, including our Sun.

PLATE TECTONICS The theory that the continents and oceans of the earth are riding on huge plates several miles thick and thousands of miles wide. The plates are slowly moving as molten rock in the earth's interior flows, pulling them along. Earthquakes and volcanoes usually occur near places where the plates move against each other.

POTENTIAL ENERGY The energy stored in an object because of its position or structure. A stretched rubber band has potential energy; the more stretch, the greater the potential energy (until it snaps!). Objects store this energy until it is released in the form of kinetic energy. (See Kinetic Energy.)

PROTEIN A large, complex molecule essential to life. Muscle and blood consist largely of protein, and enzymes are proteins. Proteins include the element nitrogen.

PROTIST A one-celled organism with a visible nucleus. According to a common classification scheme, protists constitute one of five kingdoms of life. The amoeba is probably the best-known protist. Slime molds and some kinds of algae are also protists.

QUADRUPED An animal with four feet.

QUANTUM (plural **QUANTA**) Electromagnetic and radiant energy come in quanta, which are tiny "packets" of energy. Each quantum is the smallest amount of energy that can exist. Quantum mechanics is a branch of physics that explains the structure and motion of subatomic particles.

QUASAR A celestial object larger than the largest stars but smaller than a galaxy. Quasars emit powerful blue light and, usually, radio waves. They emit thousands of times more energy than entire galaxies.

RADIO WAVE One of the kinds of electromagnetic radiation. Like all electromagnetic radiation, radio waves travel at the speed of light, but unlike many others, they have very long wavelengths and can pass through dense materials that block light.

RADIOACTIVITY The tendency of certain atoms to give off energy as their nuclei break down, a natural process called radioactive decay. The released energy comes in the form of tiny particles (called alpha and beta particles) and penetrating gamma rays that can be damaging to organisms. Radium and uranium are naturally occurring radioactive elements. There are also 13 human-made radioactive elements. (See Transuranium Element.)

REFLECTION The bouncing back of light or other energy waves when they hit a surface. A mirror reflects light while ordinary glass lets most of it pass through. When sound waves reflect, they produce an echo.

REPRODUCTION The ability of living things to produce other living things similar to themselves. Sexual reproduction involves the joining of male and female gametes. Asexual reproduction involves only one parent, who produces genetically identical offspring. Asexual reproduction occurs mostly in plants and protists.

RESPIRATION The important chemical reaction that takes place inside cells, in which oxygen is used to release energy from food. This reaction produces carbon dioxide as a waste product. In mammals (including humans), oxygen is obtained by breathing. For this reason, respiration also refers to the act of breathing.

REVOLUTION The motion one body makes around another. Usually applied to planets moving around the Sun or moons moving around their planet. One complete revolution of the earth around the Sun is called a year.

ROTATE To turn around an object's own center, or axis. A tire rotates around its center, and the earth rotates on its axis. Not to be confused with revolution. The earth revolves around the Sun once in a year, and rotates around its axis once in a day.

SOLID One of the three common states of matter (the others being gas and liquid). A solid has a definite shape and size, but when heated, it can melt and turn into a liquid. (A few solids, like dry ice, go directly from the solid to the gaseous state.)

SPECTRUM The series of colors (red, orange, yellow, green, blue, indigo, and violet—in that order) produced when white light is refracted, or bent, as when passing through a prism. A rainbow is a natural spectrum, produced by water droplets that act as tiny prisms.

SUBATOMIC PARTICLE Any of the tiny particles or packets of energy that make up atoms or are produced in nuclear reactions. Protons, neutrons, and electrons are the best-known subatomic particles. Protons and neutrons seem to be made of quarks, which are also subatomic particles. There are over a hundred others, but many exist for only a fraction of a second.

SUPERNOVA A star that suddenly enlarges and becomes millions of times brighter than it was, then dies. In one day, a supernova can give off as much energy as our Sun does in one million years!

TERRESTRIAL Refers to land, rather than water or air. A terrestrial animal is one living on land, not in the sea.

TRANSPIRATION The loss of water through plant leaves. Plants have openings in their leaves called "stomata," which open and shut to regulate how much water can pass through. Plants in arid (dry) climates cannot afford to transpire much water so they have ways to limit the amount of water that can escape.

TRANSURANIUM ELEMENT All the elements with atomic numbers greater than that of uranium (92). The 13 known transuranium elements are human-made. Most can exist for only a fraction of a second, and all are radioactive.

TSUNAMI A large, powerful ocean wave that can cause major destruction when it hits the shore. Tsunamis can be 25 meters high or more! They are caused by underwater earthquakes or volcanoes.

TYPHOON A violent tropical storm formed over the Pacific or Indian Oceans. Typhoons formed over the Atlantic are called hurricanes.

ULTRAVIOLET (UV) Electromagnetic waves with wavelengths shorter than those of violet light but longer than those of X rays. Ultraviolet light cannot be seen by humans but can be seen by many other animals, including bees who follow ultraviolet markings on some flowers. Much UV light from the Sun is absorbed in the ozone layer of the upper atmosphere. Too much exposure to UV light can be dangerous to humans.

UNICELLULAR An organism that has only one cell. Bacteria, yeast, protists, and some algae are unicellular.

URINE A nitrogen-rich waste product that is excreted by the kidneys. It is a yellow liquid in mammals and a watery paste in birds and reptiles.

VAPOR The gaseous state of a substance that is normally solid or liquid at room temperature, created by heating a liquid. Water vapor is the gaseous state of water.

VERTEBRATE An animal with a backbone. There are five groups, or classes, of vertebrates: fish, amphibians, reptiles, birds, and mammals.

VIRUS A very tiny parasite, smaller than bacteria, that invades other cells and uses its biochemical machinery to multiply. Many of them cause serious diseases in animals or plants. Human viral diseases include AIDS, flu, chicken pox, rabies, measles, and the common cold. Viruses are not killed by antibiotics, which act on bacteria, but vaccinations have been developed to prevent some viral diseases. Viruses are generally not considered living things.

WARM-BLOODED An animal that must maintain a constant, or nearly constant, body temperature regardless of the temperature of its environment. Birds and mammals are warm-blooded. "Homeo-thermic" and "endothermic" are synonyms for warm-blooded. See also Cold-Blooded.

WAVE In physics, a regularly vibrating motion or a changing electro-magnetic field that travels through air, water, or some other medium (or, in the case of electromagnetic waves, through a vacuum), and in which energy is transferred from one particle to another without causing any permanent change in the medium. Sound and light both travel as waves.

WAVELENGTH The distance between two consecutive waves of energy. It is usually measured from the peak (or trough) of one wave to the peak (or trough) of the next. The range of wavelengths in electromagnetic waves is enormous. AM radio waves have wave-lengths that are tens of meters, while visible light has wavelengths that are billionths of a meter.

WORK In physics, a transfer of energy due to a force being applied to a body. Work can involve making something move or heating it up.

X RAY Invisible electromagnetic waves with wavelengths shorter than those of light. They can penetrate human body tissues and bones and make images on photographic paper that are useful in showing breaks or other abnormalities in the body. They can also be used to study the structure of materials. X rays are emitted by many celestial bodies and they can give astronomers a great deal of information that could not be obtained using ordinary telescopes.

YEAR The time it takes a planet to make one complete revolution around its star. Also known as a solar year. If you want to be exact, a solar year on Earth is 365 days, 5 hours, 48 minutes, and 45.5 seconds. If you don't need to be so exact, just say it's $365\frac{1}{4}$ days.

YES! What scientists say when their experimental results support their hypothesis!

YOLK The yellow substance inside a bird or reptile's egg. It serves as food for the developing embryo, and is therefore rich in fat and protein.

ZENITH The point in the sky that is directly overhead. If you stood at the North Pole, the North Star would almost be at the zenith. (We say "almost" because the North Star is found close to, but not exactly at, true north.)

ZERO GRAVITY Also called freefall. The condition where no gravity can be felt, as in an orbiting spacecraft.

ZYGOTE The cell that results when a sperm cell fertilizes an egg cell. Also called a "fertilized egg." Since sperm and egg cells each have half the normal number of chromosomes, the zygote has the full number of chromosomes. It will develop into a new organism containing genes from both parents.

Index